The LOST
SHIPWRECK of PAUL

ROBERT CORNUKE

THE LOST SHIPWRECK OF PAUL
Copyright © 2003 by Robert Cornuke
Published by Global Publishing Services
ISBN 0-9714100-3-8

Cover design by Kirk DouPonce, UDG|DesignWorks, Sisters, Oregon
Interior design by Katherine Lloyd, The DESK, Bend, Oregon

Unless otherwise indicated, Scripture quotations are from:
The Holy Bible, New King James Version
© 1984 by Thomas Nelson, Inc.

Other Scripture quotations are from:
New American Standard Bible® (NASB)
© 1960, 1962, 1963, 1968, 1971, 1972, 1976, 1975, 1977, 1995
by The Lockman Foundation. Used by permission.

Global Publishing Services
P.O. Box 7956
Bend, OR 97708-7956
Toll free: 1.866.554.2665

For more information go to www.baseinstitute.org

Library of Congress Control Number: 2003103212

DEDICATED TO
THE MEMORY OF TONY

CONTENTS

The Maltese sailors love storms.

Their faces betray their love for the sea.

They are hardened to its fitful ways,

for their lives, like those of any islanders,

are wedded to the seaways.

—RICHARD WALTER

PROLOGUE

THE SOUTHEAST COAST OF MALTA—1971

A ripening sun lifted off the horizon as they rounded Zonqor Point, their weathered boat cutting through the choppy sea toward the reef where the big groupers swam. Ray sat in the back of the skiff, his small hand gripping the throttle of the sputtering two-stroke outboard motor. Ray kept his eyes fixed on his mentor and teacher in the front of the boat, who was preparing the cylinders and weight belts for the dive. Ray secretly idolized Tony, who was known throughout the island of Malta as a great diver. Tanned, bronzed, and strong, in the pecking order of local spear fishermen, Tony stood apart.

Ray's friends told him that he was too young, that it was too dangerous to dive the deep waters along the reef. And though only fourteen, he understood the risks. He'd heard the stories of those who never surfaced again after chasing the big ones. But it didn't scare him; he knew that deep water brought bigger fish.

Ray eased his tired grip on the vibrating throttle and began a long, slow circle. He had been out to the dive spot before, but waited until Tony said "Here!" to cut the engine. Tony tossed the anchor overboard, the rattling chain slipping through his calloused fingers.

"Get my tanks," he said, gazing down as the anchor vanished into the sea.

Slinging the harness holding the twin metal cylinders onto his broad shoulders, Tony shot a glance at young Ray, struggling silently to hoist his own heavy tanks onto his skinny frame. Tony reached out a hand to help. Ray leaned away, embarrassed, and then quickly wrestled the weight belt up around his waist, cinched his equipment tight, and in perfect sync with Tony, spit into his mask, smearing saliva across the glass to keep it from fogging during the dive. They popped the hard rubber regulators into their mouths, cradled their spearguns against their chests, and rocked softly backward off the gunwales and into the sea.

The pressure of the heavy tanks on Ray's shoulders eased as he felt himself gliding down slowly into a weightless, indigo blue world of dancing bubbles and piercing shafts of sunlight. As his body plunged into the clear Mediterranean, Ray savored the cool splash of water flooding his senses. Down here all was quiet, except for the hiss of air flowing in and out of the regulator. The water chilled and darkened as they swam deeper along the rocky sides of the big reef.

Nearer the bottom, Ray and Tony eased their pace, maneuvering through jagged crags and swaying seaweed, looking for the slow shadowy forms of feeding groupers. As much as Ray loved these deepwater outings, he understood that they were serious business. The big fish brought good money from the island restaurants, but it was no easy task. Ray had speared groupers before and compared it to roping a bull. If you didn't spear it square between the eyes, the fish would drag you.

One forty-pounder had pulled Ray for over thirty meters before curling itself in a deep cave, where it opened its gills and wedged itself tight. When a big grouper wedges itself thick, it is very hard to pull it free.

Tony had helped many divers in such predicaments; typically he would swim in after the fish, following the line through the narrow, rocky passageway. Pulling himself into the consuming darkness, he would feel for the metal spear still lodged in the wounded fish. Then he'd slide his hand into the grouper's gills and yank it free, dragging it out of the cave where it would be easily killed. Tony didn't consider this a risky maneuver, only a simple solution to a frequent problem. Hours later, some appreciative tourist would look at a steaming plate of grouper set in front of him and never imagine what someone had done to secure his delectable entrée.

Stroking silently along the reef, Tony stopped suddenly. He saw a grouper—big, brown, with brassy spots and huge jaws—slipping over a rock, trailing a small fish through the seaweed. With one swift, powerful thrust, the grouper pounced on its prey. Tony reached down and carefully pulled the rubber tubing along the speargun shaft and cocked the gun. He didn't bother to signal Ray, who saw what was going on and knew to keep his distance.

Groupers are voracious, violent feeders. A meal for a big one like this is anything that moves or that can fit in its mouth. Chomping down on its kill, however, it little knew that a spear was aimed at its skull. With a spray of bubbles, the spear lance exploded from Tony's speargun, glanced off a rock, and spiraled to a stop on the seabed below. *He had missed.* Tony could hardly believe his eyes as the grouper shot off into the shadows of a nearby cave. Above him, Ray cringed, knowing Tony's anger at missing such a big one.

Wasting no time, Tony arched downward, his muscular legs kicking hard toward the seafloor, wanting only to retrieve the wasted spear and resume the hunt. Reaching for the spear, he examined its newly bent tip and then turned, disgusted, to swim off. And that's when *he saw it*. From the corner of his eye, he saw a mysterious bulky form half-covered in the swaying seaweed. Tony fanned his gloved hand at the form, and as the swirl of sand settled, Ray could see it too. Swimming closer to get a better view, Ray's heart skipped a beat. Lying before him was a big, dark object covered in crustaceans. Unsheathing his knife, Tony scraped off a chip, revealing the dull glint of metal.

After belonging to the sea for almost two thousand years, this ancient object now belonged to them. ⚓

Chapter One

TWENTY-NINE
YEARS LATER

LAKE TANA, ETHIOPIA—APRIL 2000

I stepped from the darkness of the tombs, which were perched high on some jagged cliffs. My research team had just been shown some crumbling old manuscripts and skeletons of Ethiopian kings and now found ourselves squinting into the blinding, oppressively hot sun. As my eyes fought to adjust, I could just make out the captain's form waving at me far below in the tiny inlet.

It was late—far later than I promised the boat captain—and we still had several hours to cross the forty or so miles of Lake Tana to get from this remote island to the port city of Bahar Dar. The captain kept shouting at us, but we couldn't make out what he was saying. I made my way down from the cliffs through a tangled thatch of trees, along a narrow footpath, and beneath a gauze canopy of spiderwebs spread across the branches. I looked up to see thick vines infested with hundreds of scurrying, long-legged spiders roused from their sun-baked lethargy.

Ducking underneath the dangling webs, our group made its way along the ridge, where I could finally see the boat captain pacing back and forth across the bow, rubbing nervous hands over his sweat-smeared face. He glanced up to see us.

"We GO! We GO!" he screamed, waving wildly at the horizon. I looked to see a small front gathering in the distance.

Our group hurried down the narrow path, stepping cautiously on rocks worn slick and round by centuries of barefooted monks padding up and down the hand-hewn stairs. Within five minutes we'd reached the lagoon, hands on our knees, panting for air. The captain didn't intend to give us even a moment's rest.

"We GO! We GO!" he kept shouting.

With my backpack slung across my shoulder, I slid down the last steps to the rickety dock and our waiting boat. The fifty-year-old rusty-hulled, forty-foot government schooner wasn't much to look at, much less *sail* in. It had an old clattering engine that made loud exploding noises and belched thick black diesel smoke. I tossed my pack to the Ethiopian lad who served as a sort of first-mate to the captain, and we all climbed aboard. Even before I could stuff my bags below, the captain gunned the engine while my friends cast off the bow and stern lines. Within moments we were chugging into open water across the vast lake.

I still wasn't sure what had gotten the captain so worked up, but he seemed to be coming unglued, his expression betraying raw fear. Then I stared up at the western horizon and swallowed hard: The small front had now grown into an enormous, swollen bank of white-gray thunderheads mushrooming heavenward. Within its deep malevolent greens and purples, I saw the first pulsing stabs of lightning.

I'd seen these storms on prior trips to Ethiopia—and wished I hadn't. Forming silently in the moist heat swirling over the jungles and lakes, at dusk the currents would clash with the cool air in the upper atmosphere, stirring up some lethal storms. A year earlier, I'd been stranded on neighboring Tana Kirkos Island during the most ferocious storm I'd ever endured. It ripped across the island, flooding everything and nearly blowing our camp off the cliffs. To get hit by one of those on the open water was unthinkable, but by the looks of those clouds, it was already upon us.

The storm advanced quickly, the wind gaining speed as a wall of inky black swallowing up the last patches of blue sky. I didn't kid myself that we could out-run it; the clouds swirled and surrounded us, as if bent on destruction. By nightfall the swells had begun pounding against the boat—angry, rolling whitecaps hammering the rusty metal hull, lifting the bow out of the water, then slamming its nose headlong into the surf. The rain felt like lead pellets against our faces, driven down and then horizontal by the gathering gale, with only lightning breaking through the consuming darkness.

My research team—Ray Ardizzone, Dr. Pete Leininger, Ron Hicks, and Todd Phillips—sat huddled under an old rotting tarp they'd stretched across the deck, listening to the captain in the wheelhouse screaming frantically into a radio microphone trying to raise someone who could help. But I couldn't imagine anyone reaching us in this terrible tempest. I couldn't speak the captain's language, but had no trouble understanding what he was saying. His desperate cries for help had so far gone unanswered. (We learned later that the power at Bahar Dar had been knocked out by the storm, which we might have guessed by the pitch-black shoreline eerily invisible off our bow).

That's when we hit the rocks.

The impact threw us forward with a horrible and unforgettable sound of metal crunching upon rock. So that was the reason for the captain's erratic behavior—he knew that lying silently under the dark waters of the outer harbor sat a jagged reef of sharp rock outcroppings hard enough to see in broad daylight but impossible to navigate in a dark storm. The boat's metal hull ripping against the rocks created a megaphone effect that exploded in our ears—as if the boat itself shrieked out in pain. The hull climbed the rocks, shredding metal and causing the boat to list sideways. Then we heard—and felt—the grinding clatter of propeller blades smashing against the rocks, shearing and shattering. The captain, still screaming into the boat's radio, started to reverse gears but immediately snapped off the last bits of propeller, leaving the boat tilting and without traction.

Plumes of diesel smoke swirled around us, and from below deck someone shouted that we were taking on water. That's when it suddenly struck me that we might soon sink, only three-and-a-half miles from shore. My next thought was, *Maybe we could swim it.* Though in these stormy waters it would be the last resort.

Just then, Misgana, my young Ethiopian guide, sat down beside me and calmly read my thoughts. Staring blankly into the rainfall he opened his mouth and swallowed a foaming mouthful of rain.

"I'm not going to swim tonight," he said, water streaming out both sides of his mouth.

"What did you say?" I shouted over the howling wind.

Misgana leaned close, as though he didn't want the others to hear. "I was raised on this lake," he explained, "and I have sailed these waters my whole life." He stopped and stared at the heaving waves. "I know what lives in these waters. There are crocodiles. Closer to shore there are hippos, and then the snakes."

He shook his head defiantly. "No, no," he said, concluding the matter. "I prefer a pleasant death. I will hold on to this railing and go down with the boat. But I will not swim tonight."

Watching Misgana sit back against the railing and stretch out both arms in an apparent surrender to death, I knew we were in serious trouble. If Misgana, who had probably weathered a hundred of these storms, was throwing in the towel, then what hope was there? I left Misgana staring off into the darkness and went to roust the team for some earnest prayer.

So far no one on our team had begun to panic. The waves were crashing across the deck, and it seemed as if the boat might tip and founder at any moment. I asked my friend Ray to lead us in a prayer, and pray we did. We prayed for our families, we prayed for our deliverance, and then we placed the entire situation squarely in God's hands.

After several minutes, when we'd finished, we turned our attention to the problem at hand—a badly damaged and sinking ship. Just then a small dot of yellow light appeared some three hundred yards off the bow, bobbing violently in the wall of darkness. It disappeared then reappeared, disappeared then reappeared in fitful rhythm with each careening swell— when, a few minutes later, we saw the source of the light. Struggling mightily against the waves, propelled by a sputtering, five-horsepower engine, bobbed a fifteen-foot open-hulled aluminum fishing boat. The boat was so small and the swells so big that it kept vanishing into the troughs and reappearing on the top of each mounting whitecap.

It felt like forever, but the fishing skull finally reached the undertow of our rock outcropping. One of our young Ethiopian crew members took his rope and pulled them toward our bow. We swiveled a spotlight to see the weather-beaten skiff, piloted by three fishermen in rain slickers, bib rain pants, and rubber boots. Two of them used a ten-foot pole to push the boat through the perilous rocks, finally pulling alongside our crippled craft, where we could smell the potent stench of rotting fish from fishing nets that filled the small boat.

Within the hour we had safely reached shore, all of us enjoying our comfortable ride on the cushioned pile of fishing nets and cork floats. Once on shore, the fishermen confirmed our near-death experience; they told us they were returning to shore after a hard day of fishing when they barely saw the light from our boat. Well acquainted with the rocky reefs in the Bahar Dar channel, they saw that our boat was stranded and headed back into the storm to rescue us.

For me, for my crew, and for Misgana, the experience would be etched indelibly on our memories. A day later we returned to Addis Ababa to catch our flights home. Cruising away from the African continent, high over the Atlantic, I got up and grabbed my Bible from the overhead compartment. I was curious to see what I might find. I'd just spent two weeks in Ethiopia researching for a book project called *In Search of the Lost Ark of the Covenant*. In the process, I had survived a deadly storm and shipwreck. What, I wondered, was God trying to teach me in all this?

For the next several hours, I flipped through my Bible under a small beam of light. I found myself in the book of Acts, thumbing slowly to chapter 27 and the story of another shipwreck. Here Luke narrates the story of Paul, who while traveling to Rome on a large cargo vessel, ended up shipwrecked off the coast of Malta. The shipwreck story is amazingly detailed, describing everything from the vessel's nautical headings to the ship's direction of drift in the storm. The narrative goes on to explain weather patterns, duration at sea, geographic landmarks, reef configurations, sea depths, how the men onboard reacted, and how the life of every man onboard—including Paul's—was spared.

I assumed, from repeated readings of those passages, that I knew the story fairly well. But as I reread it this night over the eastern Atlantic, my eyes kept returning to one verse: "And fearing that we might run aground somewhere on the rocks, they cast four *anchors* from the stern and wished for daybreak" (Acts 27:29).

Then, reading further, I stopped at the words: "And casting off the anchors, they left them in the sea..." (v. 40).

I kept returning to those eight words:

...four anchors.
...they left them in the sea....

I wondered, rereading these dimly lit pages, if the story from Acts was calling to me across the ages. I couldn't keep my mind from going where it wanted to go—where it had gone many times before. It wasn't that I particularly wanted, or needed, to venture down this path, but the same curiosity that drove me to spend a good portion of my adulthood researching the mysteries of the Bible kicked in again. Experience had proven to me time and again that history had left behind subtle clues to validate many amazing biblical stories and that most of those clues were contained in the Bible itself. At thirty-nine thousand feet, I asked myself a couple of seemingly simple questions: *Could those anchors mentioned in Acts 27 survive all this time? And if they did, could I find them?* ⚓

Chapter Two

MISSION MALTA

COLORADO SPRINGS, COLORADO—MAY 2000

*J*thought long and hard before throwing myself headlong into a search for Paul's sea anchors. I'd spent much of the past two decades searching the world over for lost locations of the Bible, and one adventure matched another only in the monumental amounts of energy, time, and resources required. In turn, I'd been arrested five times in the Middle East, dodged bullets, fallen off glaciers, crash-landed in airplanes, and been chased by military patrols in the middle of the night. And then, of course, the shipwreck in Ethiopia. After every trip, I seemed to find myself asking, *Why do it?* The answers to this question varied with each quest, but all could be traced back to a single day in 1985 when I met a man named Jim Irwin.

Some people are fortunate enough to have a person in their lives that helps them find their true passion, or launches them off in new and exciting directions. For some it's a teacher, for others a coach, for others a parent. For me it was Jim Irwin, the lunar module pilot of *Apollo 15* and

23

the eighth man to walk on the moon. On July 26, 1971, he sat strapped into the nose cone of a *Saturn V* rocket, 360 feet in the air. After many years of NASA training, Colonel James B. Irwin, Colonel David R. Scott, and Major Alfred M. Worden watched as the capsule door slammed shut. Jim recalled how slowly the time passed until the final few seconds before liftoff—*"Four...three...two...one..."* He slid his feet tightly into the stirrups and tensed his back against the pad of his seat. When flight control said *"Ignition!"* he felt the awesome power of the engines explode to life beneath him, and the tremendous release of the rockets' fury sent a violent vibration through the bulkhead, through Jim's seat, and through his body. He said he felt the sensation of moving upward as the huge craft, suspended between earth and sky, pushed away from the launchpad.

Jim knew that if they cleared the tower things would be okay. If they didn't clear, it meant a malfunction or system failure had occurred and the crew would—in an instant—be incinerated. On that liftoff, all instruments showed "GO," and the *Saturn V* cleared the tower mast and gained velocity, the G-forces pressing them down as they hurtled through the blue Florida sky toward the moon and toward history.

I met Jim several years after his moonwalk, at a time when he was gaining worldwide notoriety, not for his lunar experience but for his personal campaign to find Noah's Ark. Back then most people couldn't understand why a famous astronaut would stake his reputation on or even be *interested* in finding Noah's Ark. Jim traced his desire to do it back to his record eighteen historic hours on the lunar surface.

It happened during a rigorous battery of tasks Jim conducted while trudging through the gray dust of the lunar landscape. Raising his visor for a moment to stare back at the earth, he saw *it*. Suspended in the consuming cold and blackness of space floated a beautiful; delicate; white, green, brown, and blue orb—*earth*—alive, breathing, yet as fragile as a Christmas ornament. In that instant he said he *knew* there was a God—a Father, an all-loving, all-powerful Creator, who alone could have authored such a scene. Jim returned from space a changed man with a new purpose and goal for life.

The very next year Jim founded the High Flight Foundation and began a life of ministry, which included searching for lost locations and mysterious artifacts of the Bible. In his repeated travels to Turkey to climb Mt. Ararat, the international press corps always swarmed him.

After Jim and I struck up a friendship in 1985 and I had helped him raise some money for an expedition, he asked me to travel with him to Turkey to search for the Ark. Jim wanted me to be his bodyguard on the expedition because I was once on the SWAT team for a police department in Southern California. I agreed to go on that trip with Jim and became hooked. I now apply the investigative techniques I learned as a policeman to searching out veiled truths of biblical history.

So here I was again—only a few weeks removed from the near disaster on Lake Tana—and I couldn't stop thinking about the four anchors of Paul. I knew that heading off across the vast frontiers of biblical history and *actually locating* the lost shipwreck of Paul was a long shot. Even though many in my sphere of influence discounted the idea, I nevertheless decided to try. I began my research, as always, in university libraries and moved quickly to archaeological websites, nautical maps, bathymetric charts, specialty books, and encyclopedias on sailing.

I was soon poring over scholarly treatises on Roman maritime history, scientific commentaries on the nature of seaborne storms, and satellite charts decoding the strange meteorology of the Mediterranean. I read through the long and almost mythical history of Malta—a history of its own rich ancient lineage, a history that in many ways has no equal. Stone temples on Malta are listed amongst the oldest freestanding structures on earth, reputedly older than Stonehenge and the Pyramids. One unique temple called the Hypogeum is an archaeological masterpiece; an intricate underground structure carved out of limestone rock using animal horns and flint.

One afternoon, my brother Paul stopped by for a visit and found me elbow-deep in maps, charts, and musty old history books about Malta. He listened politely as I explained the story of Paul's shipwreck and hinted at my quest to find the four anchors. Rubbing his chin, he bent over one of the maps and said, "Bob, this is going to be easy. There's a bay on the island of Malta called St. Paul's Bay."

Of course I knew of the bay. It was featured prominently on the maps spread out on the desk before me, known for centuries in Maltese tradition as the place of Paul's shipwreck. My brother's inference seemed to suggest I should simply travel to Malta, rent a boat, sail out on St. Paul's Bay, and find the anchors conveniently resting at the bottom of the bay. But from every search I'd ever undertaken, I knew that it's *never* that easy. But a search has to begin someplace, and St. Paul's Bay was going to be where I'd start.

MALTA—SEPTEMBER 2000

The island appeared suddenly beneath a patchwork of floating clouds as our plane made its final descent into Malta International Airport. Even from the air I immediately recognized the surrounding island features obvious on the maps I had been studying. Seen from the air, Malta *is* small, measuring only about seventeen miles at its longest distance from the southeast to the northwest, and about eight miles from east to west.

Malta sits like a shimmering gemstone in the jet blue waters of the Mediterranean, crisscrossed by beautifully terraced fields, dry creek beds and an intricate web-work of narrow roads connecting villages, medieval walled cities, and ornate, red-domed cathedrals. A band of high rugged cliffs rims the shoreline. These cliffs would make the search for the site of Paul's shipwreck considerably simpler. The Bible states that sailors aboard Paul's ship, having anchored off the coast of Malta in a near hurricane, peered out at the horizon at midnight on the fourteenth night, and:

> *They observed a bay with a beach, onto which they planned to run the ship if possible.* (Acts 27:39)

This obvious clue would help eliminate the majority of coastline of Malta. Simple deduction and the presence of those high cliffs skirting the majority of the island's perimeter would restrict the search areas to the few bays on Malta that fit the biblical narrative.

As the plane dipped for landing, I got a glimpse of St. Paul's Bay out my window, recognizable by its unique landmarks and topography. Once on the ground I wasted no time. Clearing customs, I checked into my hotel, then hailed a cab to take me to St. Paul's Bay. Within hours I stood overlooking the bay, wondering if the anchors were out there somewhere beneath the whitecaps.

St. Paul's Bay is about one mile wide at its mouth and recedes to a U-shaped inlet two miles inland. It is bordered by low-lying cliffs and rocky outcroppings, which converge on a small inlet known as Pwales

Beach. Regarding it from a sailor's point of view, I couldn't help but notice that it was only a small patch—basically nothing but a narrow stretch of sand and not really a beach at all. *The sailors could not have seen this almost unnoticable wisp of sand from two miles out to sea.* Its name and reputation aside, it didn't seem to fit the biblical narrative. Hiking around it and surveying it from above and below only reinforced in my mind that initial impression: St. Paul's Bay couldn't be what the shipwrecked sailors meant by "a bay with a beach."

I then visited the small rustic Church of the Shipwreck of St. Paul—a charming little chapel known as the traditional site where the Maltese met Paul and his companions and a large fire was lit. Built over the original site of the old church, the chapel had been bombed to rubble during WWII. Its outer walls had etchings of Bible verses describing Paul's journey to Malta and the shipwreck. Inside were paintings dating to the time of the Knights of St. John. One of the paintings portrayed Paul coming to shore after the shipwreck where he was met by a group of islanders. Among the group in the painting were two knights of St. John dressed in fifteenth-century garb.

The attending priest stood quietly at the entry. I asked him, "Is this truly the bay where St. Paul landed?"

He smiled and spoke candidly. "I'm afraid the best I can say is that this is only the *traditional* site, but we know of nothing historically that would guarantee that this is the landfall of Paul's shipwreck. As you might know," he added, "it *is* the place where they celebrate the episode of Paul from the Bible."

That was an immediate red flag. All my years of research had taught me to seriously mistrust the word *traditional*—at least as it attempts to define "traditional" sites of ancient biblical landmarks. More often than not these sites resemble precisely what I surveyed at St. Paul's Bay—scant relation to the historical scenes described—often meticulously—in the Bible. Motioning across the water toward the northwest side of St. Paul's Bay, the priest called my attention to a small rocky island located a few hundred yards off the north lip of St. Paul's Bay. A large, impressive statue of Paul was erected on its cliffs in 1854 by Salvator Borg. "Prior to the statue being built," the priest said, "the island was known as Selmunette Island. Once the huge statue was erected the island became *St. Paul's* Island." I found it a perfect illustration of how most "traditions" are born.[1]

But back to basics: The Bible speaks of the shipwreck occurring where "two seas meet." The Greek phrase *topon dithalasson* literally means "a place between waters."

> *But striking a place where two seas met, they ran the ship aground....* (Acts 27:41)

St. Paul's Island is a thin strip of rock. Its middle has the appearance of an isthmus. Here the choppy, deep waters of the Mediterranean indeed lie on one side of the small rocky island, while the placid waters of St. Paul's Bay lie on the other. It gives an initial impression of a place where "two seas meet."

Still pointing, the priest added, "On the island where the statue of Paul stands is the exact spot where some say the shipwreck happened."

But this island outcropping didn't seem to fit the Bible's description either. The Bible notes how the sailors swam to shore after striking a reef.

The writer Luke describes in detail how (as the bow of the ship ran up onto the reef) the stern remained submerged in the water, finally breaking to pieces in the violence of the waves. Even from shore I could see that if the front part of Paul's ship truly ran aground on this part of the island—which would be difficult because of the sheer jutting rocks—the sailors would have simply climbed down the front part of the ship to the rocks.

> *But the centurion…commanded that those who could*
> *swim should jump overboard first and get to land, and*
> *the rest, some on boards and some on parts of the ship.*
> (Acts 27:43–44)

Here again, the passage seems to indicate that the crew faced quite a distance to swim to shore, desperately forced to use broken planks to float to the safety of the beach. Furthermore, to even have a chance of reaching this inlet on St. Paul's Island, a ship of any size would need to make a sharp, ninety-degree right turn once it entered the outer reaches of the bay. Although no expert in maritime shipping, I knew enough from books to understand that a square-rigged sailing vessel, equipped with only two rudders (as the Bible describes the Alexandrian grain ship) would never be able to make a ninety-degree turn in a small area in a fierce storm and strike the rocks as the Bible describes.

> *And they let go the anchors and left them in the sea,*
> *meanwhile loosing the rudder ropes; and they hoisted*
> *the mainsail to the wind and made for shore.* (v. 40)

There remained another good reason for dismissing St. Paul's Bay as the shipwreck site. Luke notes that even though the sailors could clearly *see* the bay and the beach in front of them, they didn't recognize the land.

> *When it was day, they did not recognize the land. But*
> *they observed a bay with a beach....* (v. 39)

In 218 B.C., the Romans occupied Malta and made Mdina/Rabat their capital. The bay now known as St. Paul's Bay, as well as the bay immediately south of it—Salina Bay—would have been the two nearest safe harbors for Roman ships to anchor. Evidence proves that Salina Bay was used as a Roman port. Malta itself was well visited as a hub of trade during the time of the Roman occupation and would have been known to any seasoned sailor plying the Mediterranean. The Bible says that there were *276 men* on Paul's ship, and a large contingent of those men would have been sailors. With Salina Bay, and Saint Paul's Bay right next to it (with clearly recognizable cliffs and distinct shoreline features) not even a storm could have confused the sailor's sightings. Yet Luke makes it clear that only *after* the shipwreck did the sailors realize they had struck Malta.

> *Now when they had escaped, they then found out that*
> *the island was called Malta.* (Acts 28:1)

As I had seen time and time again, the Bible itself served as my guiding proof text, effectively eliminating St. Paul's Bay as the true location of the shipwreck. History had long established that Valletta, and most certainly Salina Bay next to St. Paul's Bay, were active Roman ports at the time of Paul's journey; all sat in close proximity to each other on the northern coastal area of Malta,[2] any of which would have easily been recognizable to the well-traveled sailors of that era.

Over the years, many people searching for evidence of Paul's shipwreck have scoured Saint Paul's Bay and its immediate vicinity. None, however, has done such an exhaustive search as an expedition by a group called Specialists Archaeological Systems. In 1988 this team conducted a costly and detailed archaeological and hydrographic survey of St. Paul's Bay and the surrounding area. Using a high-tech survey vessel with side-scan sonar, a sub-bottom profiler, proton magnetometer, and a microwave signal position-fixing system, this prestigious group of experts did a grid search of the area in question. The survey vessel followed a dive team spaced eight to ten meters apart.[3]

Their thorough search and detailed report revealed no archaeological finds that could be traced to the shipwreck of Paul.[4]

Several other traditional sites for Paul's shipwreck have been proposed—all in and around the general vicinity of St. Paul's Bay. In short, the other sites on the northern coastal area of Malta failed as possible candidates for locating where Paul and 275 others shipwrecked and swam to shore over nineteen centuries ago. St. Paul's Bay and adjoining coastal areas were simply very poor possibilities for the site. Every known fact and physical trait recorded in the Bible seemed to put the shipwreck location elsewhere—*but where?* ⚓

Chapter Three

A Tradition Is Born

*U*nder the right circumstances, a tradition can very quickly become "fact," which is why every culture is peppered with legends and traditions borne of false information and skewed assumptions. Take the movie *Gladiator* for example (filmed, interestingly enough, in Malta). In one dramatic scene we see a young emperor standing before a screaming crowd and stretching out his hand, finally pointing his thumb upward—a signal signifying life rather than death for a victorious gladiator. Since the movie audience assumes this tradition is true, the film becomes historical accuracy.

But *is* it true? Did the Roman emperors really use the thumbs-up gesture to indicate life, or the thumbs-down to signify death? Back in the nineteenth century, French artist Jean Leongerome made an oil-on-canvas painting of an emperor giving the thumbs-down signal to a gladiator, giving the impression that he should kill his fallen opponent. The painting was widely exhibited from 1873 onward and eventually spawned the popular notion that Roman rulers routinely signaled their intentions in the gladiatorial arena with just such a thumbs-up or thumbs-down signal. As simply as that, the painting became historical accuracy, and a new tradition was born.

The problem is, the truth differs considerably from the tradition. Another document from the end of the first century A.D. reveals a completely different meaning for the emperor's hand signals. As it turns out, if the Romans wanted the ruler to signal the death of a defeated gladiator, they probably turned their thumbs toward their chests, indicating that they wanted the victor to thrust his sword into the poor guy lying on the ground. On the other hand, if they wanted him to live, they pointed their thumbs downward to tell the soldier lower his sword and allow the loser to live.[5] In other words, the popular tradition—based on an artist's rendition—probably represented the exact opposite of historical reality.

The tradition of Paul's shipwreck occurring in "St. Paul's Bay" started in much the same way. Paul Andrew Guillaumier, a well-known Maltese historian and renowned scholar on the shipwreck of Paul, stated, "A tradition was born about Paul's shipwreck, not from historical observation but derived from a tradition more than 1200 years after the event occurred. Since Muslims had controlled the island of Malta for some time, and since the citizens were predominantly Muslim in their faith, when Christian rulers conquered Malta they needed *something*—a catalyst, an impetus—to draw people back to the faith in which the conquering authorities believed. A holy Christian site would provide that catalyst, so a church was built on what we now know as St. Paul's Bay. There a tradition started that persists today."

An Eyewitness Account

With all that in mind, it struck me that tradition has been the compass used by the vast majority in their attempt to pinpoint the exact spot of Paul's shipwreck. If I were to find anchors and the shipwreck of Paul, I knew I would have to avoid centuries of tradition and follow the Bible.

I began studying the writings of Luke, a proven historian of the highest caliber, who according to the vast majority of scholars was the person who actually stood on the deck of the Alexandrian grain freighter and witnessed the events of Acts 27. Luke describes in graphic detail the storm, the ship's route, the sailors' actions, and the topography of the shoreline, even the depth of the water where the ship's anchors were finally abandoned.

It's hard not to admire a historian like Luke. Time and time again he has proven the critics wrong.

As every police officer knows, eyewitness accounts rank as the best source of information. In an investigation or a court of law, nothing counts more than the testimony of someone who was actually there—at the scene. The dramatic moment in any trial comes when a witness gives his or her eyewitness testimony, then points directly at the defendant and says, "He's the one. He did it."

That's why Luke's account is so important to the search for the anchors. He experienced that horrifying ordeal at sea and wrote about it in detail. In his own words we can hear him today, "This is what happened, and here is the exact spot where it happened." I needed to delve into every word of Luke's account and find the clues he left. I needed to find that exact bay and that exact spot on the seafloor he had described so long ago.

THE VOYAGE AND STORM

The events leading up to Paul's voyages are well documented in Acts. Paul had been wrongly accused by the Jews in Jerusalem and then arrested by the Romans, who had him transferred to the seaside city of Caesarea to await trial. After two years of sitting in a wretched prison cell, he was given his right as a Roman citizen to appeal to Caesar's court. The prisoner Paul was sent with a shipment of other prisoners from Judea to Rome.

According to Luke, the voyage began with the prisoners from Caesarea being placed in the charge of a Roman officer named Julius. Julius not only occupied the rank of centurion—the backbone of the Roman military machine—but also was from "the Augustan cohort," an elite unit charged with palace security and royal protection in Caesarea.[6] No doubt a hardened career soldier, who had risen through the ranks of Rome's thousands of warriors to occupy an office of privilege and responsibility, Julius would have been a man not to trifle with. The moment Julius set foot onboard ship, he would have been in charge.

Julius booked passage from the port of Caesarea on a local Adramyttium vessel, probably a smaller merchant ship servicing the smaller ports along the coast of Judea, Lebanon, and Asia Minor. The early part of the voyage was routine and uneventful, as the ship put in briefly at Sidon on the Lebanese coast before setting a course for the larger hub port of Myra, located on the southern coastline of Asia Minor. According to biblical scholar F. F. Bruce, "With a steady wind from the west, the best route from Alexandria to Italy was by Myra, which was in fact one of the chief ports serving the grain-fleet."[7]

Myra was a substantial port, bustling with activity and large enough to service the enormous ships carrying goods in and out of the harbor. According to the Bible, the vessel they had been sailing on would not be available to take them on to Italy, so in Myra the centurion needed to find another ship to transport them the rest of the way to Rome. In those days, the centurion probably would have walked along the seafront and simply inquired about ships able to take on passengers traveling west to the empire's capital. Passenger ships did not exist in the first century, so travelers needing to cover long distances by sea would need to find a trade or cargo ship and then wait for a scheduled departure date.

An obvious choice would have been one of the huge Alexandrian grain freighters that regularly sailed from Egypt to Rome. Bruce writes, "The transport of grain from Egypt, the chief granary of Rome, was of the highest importance: the shipping fleet devoted to it was organized for the service of the Roman state 'as early as the Ptolemaic period.'"[8]

The Alexandrian freighters that were assigned the overwhelming task of feeding Rome had to be the biggest, safest, and fastest ships of their day, an elite class all their own. The ancient historian Philo wrote of these grand vessels: "The ships are crack sailing craft, and their skippers the most experienced there are; they drive the vessels like racehorses on an unswerving course that goes straight as a die."[9]

It was autumn, late in the sailing season, when the centurion booked passage for himself, his soldiers, and the captives. The weather patterns could be troublesome in the fall, but the helmsman felt they would have no problem getting the rest of the way to Rome.

Aside from a few pottery and graffiti etchings in catacombs and caves, we have very little to tell us what these grain freighters actually looked like. Fortunately, around the middle of the second century, an essayist named Lucian provided a description of a grain freighter. It seems an

Alexandrian grain freighter was driven off course by a storm and took refuge in Piraeus, the port of Athens. Athens had, by the second century, long lost its power and importance as world center and was now nothing more than a simple university town. So when a massive Alexandrian freighter anchored in the harbor, crowds of people flocked to the waterfront to see it. Lucian records the event as follows:

> What a size the ship was! One hundred and eighty feet in length, the ship's carpenter told me, the beam more than a quarter of that, and forty-four feet from the deck to the bottom, the deepest point in the bilge. What a mast it had, what a yard it carried, what a forestay held it up! The way the sternpost rose in a gradual curve with a gilded goose-head set on the tip of it, matched at the opposite end by the forward, more flattened, rise of the prow with the figure of Isis, the goddess the ship was named after, on each side! And the rest of the decoration, the paintings, the red pennant on the main yard, the anchors and capstans and winches on the foredeck, the accommodations toward the stern—it all seemed like marvels to me! The crew must have been as big as an army. They told me she carried so much grain that it would be enough to feed every mouth in Athens for a year.[10]

Two hundred and seventy-six men, including Paul and Luke, boarded the ship on which Julius booked passage. According to the Bible, the owner, helmsman, centurion, soldiers, sailors, prisoners, and a large cargo of grain filled the ship. Sailing for Rome along a course that took them by the customary route toward the port of Cnidus, they soon ran into difficult headwinds and had no choice but to turn south and shadow the coast of Crete in order to continue making westward progress. As we read in Luke's account, "The wind not permitting us to proceed, we sailed under the shelter of Crete off Salmone" (Acts 27:7).

Rounding Cape Salmone on the southeast corner of Crete, they put into port at the first convenient harbor on Crete's southern coast—Fair Havens. Here a debate arose among the centurion, the captain, the helmsman, and Paul. They argued whether they should stay in the port of Fair Havens for the winter or risk the unpredictable weather and sail along the south coast of Crete to a harbor known in the first century as Phoenix. Phoenix was apparently a port better suited for waiting out the winter months, and the centurion listened to the helmsman and the owner of the ship and not to Paul. Paul sternly warned them that there would be loss of life, ship, and cargo if they went out to sea again. Jefferson White writes, "According to the Roman historian Seutonius, throughout this era the city of Rome faced continuing shortages of food during the winter months. Thus the Emperor Claudius offered substantial bonuses to ship owners who took the chance of sailing late in the season."[11]

Departing Fair Havens, they sailed along the southern coast of Crete: "When the south wind blew softly, supposing that they had obtained their desire, putting out to sea, they sailed close by Crete" (Acts 27:13).

The ship hugged the south shore of the island of Crete and was probably rounding Cape Matala as a favorable south wind gave them full canvas. The prow of the massive grain ship must have peeled an impressive wake through the calm seas as the island of Crete slowly passed by off the starboard side. The decision to press on looked like a good choice after all. But suddenly, in an instant that would define history, the wind changed. The ship's rigging slackened as the sails fluttered in confusion. Dark black rain-gorged clouds spilled over the mountain peaks of Crete and raced down toward them. The sailors knew immediately that a "Euroclydon," a violent northeaster, was about to hit. And it struck fear in their hearts.

> *But not long after, a tempestuous head wind arose, called Euroclydon.* (v. 14)

Like sailors today, ancient mariners held deep superstitions, refusing even to board a ship if someone had a bad dream about an impending journey. Now, sailing into the storm's deadly path, they certainly remembered Paul's grave warning that the voyage would end in a disaster, with a great loss to cargo, ship, and all onboard. Persuaded instead by the owner and the helmsman of the ship, Julius the centurion had ignored Paul's caution and no doubt already regretted the decision.

The violent storm front smashed into the ship, and the command went out to turn the ship about and attempt to tack back into the wind and the shadow of Crete. But the full force of the gale had already blasted them. They were at the mercy of the wind, the sea, and God and were helpless to do anything but let the ship be driven away from the island of Crete: "So when the ship was caught, and could not head into the wind, we let her drive" (v. 15). The ship was then helplessly blown to the eastern edge of Clauda, a tiny island located just off the south shore of Crete.

And running under the shelter of an island called Clauda, we secured the skiff with difficulty. (v. 16)

To prevent the ship's lifeboat, which was towed closely behind, from sinking, snapping off, or ramming the grain freighter, the sailors hauled the skiff to the deck and secured it there. By then any hope of steering the ship had long since passed. The vessel's two huge wooden steering oars were pulled up and lashed to the sides so they wouldn't snap off. The sails were pulled down, and the rigging cables were then passed under the hull of the ship and were cinched tight in an attempt to keep the planking from being wrenched apart. To the added horror of the sailors, they then realized that the gale winds were blowing them southwest into the direction of the dreaded Gulf of Syrtis, on the north coast of Africa.

...and fearing that they might run aground on...Syrtis... (v. 17b, NASB)

Sailors regarded "the Syrtis" as a place of inexpressible fear. To become marooned on the shores of Syrtis's scorching hot sand would be a fate worse than drowning at sea.

So desperately dry and hot was this Libyan desert that a World War II era B-24 bomber named *Lady Be Good* turned up in the sand after being lost for sixteen years. It had no rust on its guns, and every mechanical part remained in perfect working order. In that same desert were recently discovered the mummy-like remains of a nomad and his camels, amazingly well preserved in the perfectly arid desert air after more than two hundred years of exposure.[12]

The sailors knew what lay in wait for them in Syrtis—an inescapable, vast wasteland of sun-scorched sand where they would certainly suffer a slow, waterless death. With no choice but to find a way of skirting its fatal shoreline, they dropped into the sea a type of small parachute (in some translations described as a sea anchor) to slow their rate of drift.

> They let down the sea anchor and in this way let themselves be driven along. (Acts 27:17b, NASB)

The terminology of this tactic is specific: The desperate crew employed a time-proven emergency measure, one that modern sailors have rediscovered as perhaps the best way of surviving a vicious, ship-crippling storm. The sea anchor was no doubt fashioned out of a portion of the ship's sailcloth and probably looked something like a modern windsock. This water-borne parachute was lowered into the water and trailed behind the ship like a massive underwater sail. Gradually, the anchor slowed the ship's wind-driven advance toward the Syrtis and took advantage of the drag to pull the ship ever so slightly to the starboard, veering away from the northern coast of Africa. The ship would have made a slight arching turn toward the west-northwest in the direction of Malta.

The furious Euroclydon winds continued to whip the Mediterranean into monster waves, pounding the ship and sending the 276 men onboard sliding into railings, slamming into rigging, and holding on for dear life lest they be swept from the deck into the churning sea. Though the ship was huge, there was probably little or no shelter for the soldiers, prisoners, and crew—except for perhaps the captain and a few select shipmates. The waves soaked through the deck into the hold below, contaminating the valuable cargo of grain. But the sailors by now feared for their very lives and were painfully aware that they still had unknown terrors to endure in the numbing cold and piercing rain.

The next day's light revealed a new threat. Taking on more and more water, the ship listed lower and threatened, if the storm continued, to capsize altogether.

> *And because we were exceedingly tempest-tossed, the*
> *next day they lightened the ship.* (Acts 27:18)

The men who owned and financed the huge Alexandrian grain freighters were as profit-minded as today's shippers. After stowing grain by the hundreds of tons in the bellies of their ships, they filled them on up to the gunwales with dry goods, textiles, luxuries, and anything else they could sell to affluent and middle-class Romans. Now, as the storm showed no signs of abating, everyone—crew, prisoners, soldiers—set to the almost unthinkable task of tossing as much of the cargo as possible overboard. In frantic lines they passed cargo from man to man, heaving amphora jars, sacks, bundles, and baggage to the depths of the sea, hoping to postpone the inevitable and keep a little distance between the sea and the deck that was cracking apart beneath them.

By daybreak of the third day, the situation demanded even more desperate measures:

> *On the third day we threw the ship's tackle overboard*
> *with our own hands.* (v. 19)

Leaving the grain deep in the keel for stability, they threw over the ship's rigging, tackle, and maritime equipment—but not the ship's anchors, which were spared by the dimmest hope that somehow the anchors could be used to save the men if they encountered land.

In indescribable wind, cold, and waves, all onboard stared desperately at jagged lightning shards dancing across the horizon, splitting the sky. Drifting hopelessly on, losing more cargo and rigging to the devouring tide, they gave up all hope that they would ever be saved.

> *Now when neither sun nor stars appeared for many days, and no small tempest beat on us, all hope that we would be saved was finally given up.* (v. 20)

TRUE SURVIVAL

By this stage of the journey, the men onboard with Paul had already survived an ordeal of unimaginable duration and hardship. More likely than not they suffered from advanced stages of hypothermia. Every ounce of strength had been sapped by the wet and cold; raw adrenaline and a stubborn will to live alone must have kept them hanging on in spite of the grim, unsanitary conditions. We can only imagine the awful smells, the nausea, and utter despair felt by those weary, emaciated forms staring out with sunken eyes at the unyielding, unforgiving sea.

In their panicked state, the famished men could not even stomach a mouthful of stale bread. Yet in that moment, Paul stood in the midst of them and said:

"Men, you should have listened to me, and not have sailed from Crete and incurred this disaster and loss. And now I urge you to take heart, for there will be no loss of life among you, but only of the ship. For there stood by me this night an angel of the God to whom I belong and whom I serve, saying, 'Do not be afraid, Paul; you must be brought before Caesar; and indeed God has granted you all those who sail with you.' Therefore take heart, men, for I believe God that it will be just as it was told me. However, we must run aground on a certain island." (vv. 21–26)

Finally, after fourteen nights of hopeless, interminable drifting in driving wind and rain, the men heard something. Over the wind howling against the riggings, the sailors made out the faint rumblings of waves crashing on rocks.

Now when the fourteenth night had come, as we were driven up and down in the Adriatic Sea, about midnight the sailors sensed that they were drawing near some land. (v. 27)

At the helmsman's command, a sailor struggled toward the bow and hurled a bell-shaped lead weight overboard to measure the depth of the water. The rope attached to the lead weight hissed through the sailor's hands as it plunged to the bottom of the sea. The line probably had knots tied in measured increments so that the sailor could assess the depth by the counted knots passing through his hands.

"Twenty fathoms!" shouted the sailor to the anxious helmsman, reporting a depth of 120 feet.

Fearing that the sea was becoming shallower and shallower, the helmsman immediately asked for another sounding. The second sounding marked fifteen fathoms (ninety feet). No more soundings were required. The helmsman knew that they were drawing into shallow waters, and with the waves amplified as they drew nearer and nearer to land, the command was given to drop the ship's four anchors from the stern. Somehow the sailors drew enough strength to hoist the enormous anchors with solid lead stocks over the railing and into the sea. The drifting ship held fast. After fourteen days of being helplessly blown across the sea, they were now fixed in place off the coast of Malta.

Shivering in the darkness, the weary men huddled through the night, praying for dawn to come.

UP FROM AFRICA

From this gritty life-and-death account, we can accurately retrace the ship's tortured course toward Malta. It became clear to me that Paul's ship blew off of the coast of Crete in a southwesterly direction, past the lee of Clauda, closely passing by the coast of Africa and slanting up through the Adriatic, where it eventually intersected the small island of Malta.

I had been working on my own theory, and if it was correct, the ship of Paul traveled up from the coast of Africa and met landfall on the southeastern coast of Malta. Saint Paul's Bay is located on the northeast coast and would not be encountered with this drift scenario. I scanned my nautical maps and saw only two possible bays in the south of Malta that fit with my theory. The anchors of Paul, if they still existed, would lie under approximately ninety feet of water in front of one of two bays: Marsaxlokk or St. Thomas.

I returned to my hotel on St. Paul's Bay, packed my bags, and hired a cab to drive me to the rocky southeastern seacoast and the fishing village of Marsaxlokk Bay. ⚓

Chapter Four

Marsaxlokk Bay

The cab headed to the southeast tip of Malta. The driver was so unfamiliar with the area that he stopped and asked directions. Traveling down winding streets lined with terraced vineyards and old stone-walled houses, we entered the outskirts of the seaside village of Marsaxlokk.

The cab driver knew I would need a hotel and took it upon himself to ask a woman walking down a narrow side street for directions. She balanced a big bag of groceries overflowing with flowers and two large breadsticks on her hip, all the while hanging on to a squirming boy tugging at her hand. I asked the cab driver to please not bother her, but he dismissed me with the wave of a hand and leaned out the window, muttering something in Maltese. I assumed it was a request for information about a possible hotel in the area, and sure enough she answered in English, turning to look up the road to say simply, "The Golden Sun Hotel." She paused a moment and added, "It is the only hotel in the village." Raindrops started to lightly fall. She looked up, paused, then turned away and hurried up the street, shifting the bundle on her hip and towing the young boy behind her.

We drove to the Golden Sun Hotel, where I checked in, stowed my gear, and promptly exited down a side street to Marsaxlokk Bay. The rain had increased, but my curiosity had gotten the better of me. I couldn't wait to check out the fishing village before the gathering storm opened up. Strolling past tiny blocks of yellow stone buildings, patina-stained by years of curing in the salty sea air, I found Marsaxlokk to be a quaint Mediterranean-style fishing village. Charming two-story old-world Maltese homes and small cottage restaurants rimmed the small harbor, clustered tightly with brightly colored traditional Maltese boats called *Luzzu*.

On the wharf, fishermen moored their tiny vessels and covered them with canvas tarps as the wooden boats bobbed nervously in the headwinds of a growing September storm. Restaurant owners hastily lowered bright yellow umbrellas, fighting wind gusts that threatened to blow them off their patios.

The skies opened up and sent a torrent through the narrow streets. Sheets of water gushed over the concrete seawall along the bay. Finding shelter under a restaurant tarpaulin, I found it mildly ironic that a storm in Ethiopia had put me on the scent of Malta, the storm of Paul brought me here, and now another storm greeted me.

Near shore, not far from where I stood, a returning fishermen furiously rowed his dinghy to a small dock and tied it off, quickly running across the quay to a makeshift tarp-covered curio shop a short distance away. A woman appeared and handed him a towel. Their small portable souvenir stand offered tourists trinkets and Maltese mementoes of the picturesque bay, but today Marsaxlokk Bay was not so scenic. It was cold, wet, and windy as the family boxed up their wares to take home for the night.

I assumed the man was a fisherman and made my way across the wharf to ask them if I could perhaps share the small patch of dry ground beneath their tarp. My sudden appearance startled the entire family, but I cheerfully introduced myself and soon learned the man's name was Le Li. His wife was Sue, his young daughter was Emma, and his older son was Michael.

I thought the family was Maltese, but Sue spoke with a charming British accent and sounded as if she had just stepped out of a Kensington teahouse. She explained that she had visited Malta on vacation years earlier and found the popular tourist site an unusually warm, irresistible place with mild weather. During her stay she met and fell in love with a Maltese fisherman.

A rumble of thunder rolled across the blustery bay.

"The storm will not end today," Le Li said, cinching down the flapping tarps of his souvenir stand. Sue and her two children commenced packing up the hundreds of items.

I eyed Le Li's boat, moored at the dock. "Is your boat available for charter?" I asked. "I would only need it for an hour or two."

"If you would like," Le Li answered softly, exhibiting traditional Maltese hospitality. Without questioning why I might need his boat, he said simply, "My son Michael will take you out in our boat tomorrow around four o'clock. His duties at the souvenir stand will be over then, and the boat will be available."

I thanked them, said good-bye, and returned to the Golden Sun Hotel to get dinner and some rest.

The next day, promptly at 4 P.M., I arrived back at the dock and tossed my gear onboard Le Li's small fishing boat, brightly adorned with the traditional yellow, orange, green, and blue colors of the Maltese fishing fleet. As with all the boats I saw in the harbor, two eyes had been painted on the bow. Michael said the eyes kept away evil spirits, "which is why every fisherman paints new eyes on the front of his boat every year."

I had read that the people of Malta entertained many folklores, most a by-product of countless cultures invading them over thousands of years. One of those folklores could be seen on many Maltese church fronts: two clocks shared wall space, "One," said Michael, "to tell the people when to worship, the other to trick the devil."

Le Li had come to see us off. He cast off the lines, shoved the boat away from the dock with his foot, and watched us drift away. The diesel engine sputtered to life, and Michael slid the throttle forward, steering us out past dozens of moored fishing boats into a glaring sun in a cloudless sky. The sea breeze felt good against my skin as Michael increased the boat's speed, the loud, thumping diesel humming in our ears.

Michael wasted no time at all in showing off his tour guide skills, calling out various landmarks. He pointed toward shore in the inner bay and pronounced, "That's where two Turks were dug up."

"Two Turks? What do you mean?"

"Recently the rain and wind eroded some dirt that was covering skeletons," Michael explained. "It turns out that the two skeletons are Turks that were buried there in 1565, after the Great Siege."

Michael explained that the Great Siege of Malta ranks as the second most famous event in Maltese history (the first is Paul's visit). In 1565, the Ottoman army of Suleyman the Magnificent landed in Marsaxlokk Bay, where some say as many as forty-thousand Turkish soldiers in 180 ships intended to annihilate all those he called the "sons of dogs."

Suleyman attacked Malta and, in a four-month battle that witnessed some of the bloodiest fighting ever recorded in the annals of war, laid deadly siege to the tiny island. The outnumbered Knights of St. John, who fought the invaders alongside the able-bodied men and women of Malta, defended Malta. One of the biggest battles occurred at Fort St. Elmo, where the Knights poured burning oil on the Turks before the fort finally fell. The Turks tortured the surviving handful of wounded knights, nailed them to crosses, and floated them out of the grand harbor in Valletta.

The battle became known throughout the world as the Great Siege of Malta. Eventually the knights won a great victory, and the Turks were forced to retreat. "It appears that before they left the island," Michael told me, "the Turks buried some of their dead in shallow graves along Marsaxlokk Bay.

Motoring by the empty graves at the water's edge, I imagined two young Turkish men traveling across a vast sea to fight on an island they knew little about. They would've been forgotten in history but for the happenstance of erosion from some recent rain. It wouldn't be until Napoleon landed in Marsaxlokk bay in 1798 that the end would come to the romantic era of the chivalrous Knights of St. John on the island of Malta.[13]

Malta has been ravaged by a steady stream of invaders from the far threshold of recorded history. It was hard for me to imagine this quiet island as a staging ground of the horror and distruction of war. In World War II for instance, Malta experienced the heaviest bombardment (per square mile) of any country during World War II. In one month alone, over seven thousand tons of bombs were dropped on Malta. The country endured endless air raids, with a single attack lasting over thirteen hours. Forced to live underground, the Maltese sought shelter in caves, forgotten tombs, tunnels, catacombs, and abandoned dry wells. The horrors of war gripped the island, constant air attacks making it difficult to sleep or conduct business.

Thousands were killed or injured, with nearly every family on the island losing family members. Although the population of Malta suffered greatly, their bravery, courage, and resolve never faltered. Even when standing alone, facing impossible odds, they refused to surrender.

One of the most amazing stories during the World War II era is known as the "Miracle of Mosta." The story took place in the village church of Mosta, an ornately decorated church that boasts one of the largest unsupported domes in Europe. On April 9, 1942, when the air bombardments were at their worst, over three hundred people had gathered for a prayer meeting. As the congregation reverently waited for the service to begin, the air raid sirens began to scream, and the dreaded drone of bomber engines soon followed.

Suddenly, a shrill, whizzing sound was heard as a German bomb pierced through the beautiful rotunda, ripping a hole in the ceiling. The church trembled in a violent shudder as the sanctuary filled with dust and debris. With a sickening thud, the bomb landed, skidded across the cold, marble floor, and bounced against a wall before coming to a stop at the feet of the stunned congregation. Miraculously, the 535-pound bomb, which later proved to be "armed and alive," did not explode. Not a person was killed that day, and the people now call it the Miracle of Mosta.

Off the starboard a huge terminal port facility, where I had watched massive cargo ships arriving and leaving all day long, seemed to guard the mouth of the bay. Marsaxlokk Bay houses one of the largest container ports in the Mediterranean, strategically located on the main trade routes between Gibraltar and the Suez Canal. From its enormous free port, large cranes and trucks shuffle containers by the thousands, servicing more than two thousand ships a year.

Michael then said something that concerned me. He told me the sea terminal had been commissioned in the 1960s and that to prepare the shoreline for construction there had been extensive dredging in the bay. Had this dredging upset the reef or reconfigured the seafloor? I feared it might hurt my research, for the Bible clearly stated that Paul's ship, after it dropped four anchors, ran aground on a *reef* in front of a bay. Had the dredging erased crucial evidence?

With the palm of his hand, Michael nudged the throttle forward and at the same time turned the wheel to port, taking the small boat on an eastward heading. As we advanced toward the mouth of the bay, Michael pointed out the exact place where a recent famous world event occurred in Marsaxlokk Bay.

In December 1989 the Soviet Union (represented by Mikhail Gorbachev) and the United States (represented by George H.W. Bush) met in the bay to discuss ending the Cold War. Those important meetings took place aboard a large Soviet ship, the *Maxim Gorkey*. A gray angry storm, a gregale—a northeaster with gale force winds—slammed into Malta at the very time of the summit meetings. It was, to say the least, a chamber of commerce nightmare for the usually tranquil country of Malta. On television the world over people watched the violent tempest pound Marsaxlokk Bay as waves mounted to sixteen feet just outside the harbor.

Former President Bush was staying on the guided missile cruiser USS *Belknap* that was also anchored in Marsaxlokk Bay. The seas were so rough and the winds so relentless that the anchors of the huge ship dragged across the seafloor even though it was anchored in the protection of the bay. Almost all the seasoned sailors aboard those military ships were plagued with nausea. I talked to an eyewitness who was with President Bush. "The President," he told me, "was one of the few people aboard the USS *Belknap* who was not seasick. He walked the decks of the missile cruiser encouraging the green sailors hanging over the ships railings." The torential rain came down in silvery sheets, the clouds crackled with stabs of lightning, and the wind endlessly shrieked. Those assigned to protect the President tensely watched as the small transport boat ferrying president Bush between the two ships repeatedly disappeared in the depression of the sea's deep troughs. Even though the conditions were challenging, the meetings continued and the world was forever reshaped.

As Michael steered his boat from the site of that historic place, I wondered what it must have been like for Paul and his shipmates as they were caught in the claws of a similar storm. They were not in the safety of a bay, but were exposed to a frenzied, neverending, ruthless sea. Against all odds, they somehow survived.

We motored out beyond the harbor and into the open sea. The small luzzu lifted and rocked as it greeted each incoming swell, the bow of the boat sliding over the cresting sea and falling into a splash of salt-laced spray. Outside the bay I could appreciate just how small Malta is—easy to miss in the inky blackness of a nasty storm. Under certain conditions a ship might pass within a couple of miles of landfall and never even see the island perched alone in the consuming horizon of the vast Mediterranean.

If Paul's ship drifted helplessly along from the northern shore of

Africa, as I theorized, it would make landfall on the narrow stretch of coastline at the southeastern tip of Malta. This course of drift would allow only two possible landing sites for the shipwreck: the waters beneath Michael's boat in Marsaxlokk Bay or another bay named St. Thomas Bay, located a few miles north of Marsaxlokk. These two bays were the only "bays with a beach"—the primary consideration for determining the actual landfall of Paul's ship.

Michael activated his depth finder mounted under the diesel engine cowling. This gave me a firsthand chance to analyze the depths of the outer bay and compare them to the depth levels recorded by Luke in the Bible. As our boat crisscrossed over the seafloor, I quickly saw on the depth finder that the only place in the bay that possibly matched the Bible's description for the anchoring location was in the middle of the Marsaxlokk channel area at the mouth of the bay. From the deck of Michael's boat, I could see only two low-lying places on the shoreline in the inner bay, which could barely be considered beaches. This wasn't a very encouraging observation because the most crucial piece of this complicated puzzle was glaringly absent—a reef that the ship of Paul could have run aground on after the anchors were dropped and the ship made for shore and the "beach."

Even so, I could not disqualify Marsaxlokk Bay as a viable site until I had a chance to check out the depth of the seafloor topography in the bay prior to the huge terminal port's dredging and construction in the sixties. Without a reef, however, it looked like a death knell to this location, leaving me with only St. Thomas Bay to consider.

Back at the dock, Le Li greeted us while tying off the bow and stern lines. "Enjoy your trip?" he asked.

"Yes," I said. "Malta is quite beautiful."

I paid Michael for his time and for the use of the boat (and for his fascinating impromptu history lesson!).

Le Li smiled and said with a wink, "He has a girlfriend. The money, it will go fast."

With the sun now retiring behind a bank of clouds, I invited Le Li to join me for a cool drink and a meal at a nearby seaside café.

THE OLD MAN AND THE SEA

Le Li sat across from me and twirled a long strand of pasta on his plate. The balmy air was infused with the smell of the sea salt and buttered garlic steaming off the platter of mussels and fried squid before us.

With the western sky casting its cloak over the dying embers of an evening sun, I looked across the deep grays of Marsaxlokk Bay. Moments earlier, a big cargo ship had moved away from its moorings, its enormous mass visible in the outer bay, being pushed from the dock area by a straining tug. Massive propellers rotated faster and faster, churning up a boiling swirl of foam as the giant hulk groaned out into the bay.

Outside the harbor, a tiny skiff, waiting patiently for the behemoth to pass, bobbed sharply in the ship's titanic wake. From my table I could see the lights on the cargo ship's wheelhouse flicker to life as the freighter turned to the west, heading toward the Straits of Gibraltar and the Atlantic Ocean.

Le Li lifted his fork of spaghetti and casually pointed it toward the harbor. "Do you see that small boat out there?" he asked, "the one coming in? That's the oldest fisherman in the village. He's always the last fisherman in."

I stared out at the tiny skiff. "Why last?"

Le Li shrugged. "I don't know. He stays out all day and comes in at night. He stays close to the harbor, fishing the calm waters and avoiding the late afternoon winds." He stuffed a wad of pasta in his mouth. "Only problem," he added, "is that few fish are caught there these days. Still, he always goes out, day after day, never missing, except when the bad storms come."

I turned in my seat to watch the old man skillfully weave his skiff through the cluster of fishing boats moored in the inner harbor, grace-fully maneuvering all the way up to the small dock in front of our café. The other fishing boats had returned hours ago, their owners hurrying home to their waiting families, but not this old fellow.

"The old man lives alone," Le Li said, as if anticipating my thoughts. "As long as anyone can remember, he has lived by himself—no wife, no children."

The old man slowed the sputtering motor and cut the engine, gliding silently to the dock. Without looking he reached out, snagged a line, and tied off the boat, going through the endlessly repeated routine of stowing his gear and tugging an old tarp over the small engine of his boat. Watching the unhurried grace of his movements, I felt, for just an instant, envious of his seemingly stress-free life. Yet it also struck me as sad—this lonely, aged figure winding down another day in speechless solitude, alone but for the sea, the fish, and his boat.

Moving to the bow of the boat, he pulled a rope and retrieved a wire-mesh contraption containing two small crabs. From my unseen vantage, I watched him stare a few moments without expression at his measly catch, then let the trap slip back into the dark water. From the bottom of his boat he snagged two small fish, rolled them up in a crumpled newspaper, and tucked them under his left arm.

"His meal for tonight," commented Le Li, spearing a plump mussel with his fork.

Pulling his boat along a rope to the dock, the old man winced with pain as he climbed from the skiff. It was obvious his body was stiff and aching from spending an entire day on a wooden plank seat in the small boat.

"How old is he?" I asked Le Li.

"Eighty years, maybe more," he said. "No one knows for sure."

As the old man shuffled up the landing and walked by our table, I couldn't resist the urge. I stood from my seat and stopped him. He obviously knew a lot about the island, its weather, its reefs, and the currents. I wanted desperately to talk to him.

My abrupt manner seemed to distress Le Li, who had already mentioned that the old man disliked speaking to strangers. I believe he thought the old man would dismiss me entirely—but to both our surprise, the old man smiled warmly at me, sensing, perhaps in my body language, genuine and respectful sincerity.

I asked Le Li to interpret and asked the old man, "Sir, if you don't mind my asking, why do you go out every day, spending the whole day and early evening fishing?"

"I like to fish," the old man replied. His unvarnished answer seemed so obvious that I felt embarrassed for having even asked the question. I quickly recovered and got to the point: "Sir, can you tell me about Marsaxlokk Bay? I'm interested in learning about the seafloor, the *bottom*—the reefs."

He furrowed his brow, seeming confused, as if to say, "What *exactly* do you want to know?"

"The bay…" I said, pointing out to the water. "Was there a reef in the mouth of the bay before the big terminal was built?"

"No," he said, turning to face the harbor. "There was no reef in the harbor before they dredged the area."

Obviously, I hoped to establish by the old man's testimony if there had been a reef like the one the Bible clearly describes in Acts 27. This salty old fisherman knew the shoreline configuration before the heavy dredging of the 1960s altered its contours. Since Marsaxlokk Bay was the largest bay on the southeast coast of Malta, I still considered it a candidate for the shipwreck location. But, like St. Paul's Bay, some of the key reference points described by the Bible were straying off target.

I sensed the old man's impatience and sought his permission to ask one more question.

He nodded.

"At the entrance to the bay, is there a reef, a place where two seas meet?"

He thought for a moment and then said, "No reef here, but where the two seas meet in a storm would be the reef off of St. Thomas Bay—the Munxar Reef."

I had mentioned no storm, so Le Li offered to explain. "During a storm," he said, "*especially* a northeaster, the currents collide over the Munxar." He described it as a phenomenon all the fishermen know very well—a violent, continuous convergence of water extending for a mile and a half off St. Thomas Bay. Le Li smiled as he spoke, waving a final nugget of squid on his fork. "Oh yes. The wave looks like a serpent winding its way out to sea." Euphorically chewing the rubbery flesh, he chortled, "I will tell you this, mister, during a storm, *no one* goes where the two seas collide."

And they let go the anchors and left them in the sea, meanwhile loosing the rudder ropes; and they hoisted the mainsail to the wind and made for shore. But striking a place where two seas met, they ran the ship aground; and the prow stuck fast and remained immovable, but the stern was being broken up by the violence of the waves. (Acts 27:40–41)

Chapter Five

A Bay with a Beach

J woke early and made my way out of Marsaxlokk village, walking along a narrow winding road bordered on both sides by terraced fields and stacked rock walls. The sea air flooded my senses in the soothing still of a cool morning. A traditional, one-seat Maltese surrey clattered up the road alongside me, pulled by a spirited chestnut horse. The driver, hunched forward, snapped the reins against the animal's lathered neck and shot me a inquisitive grin as he passed. I waved a casual hello and did a double take when the driver jerked back the reins and, supposing I wanted to talk, stopped the horse, its hooves skidding to a wabbled stop across the slick asphalt.

For an awkward moment, I just stood there, unsure of what to say. Finally I stammered a clumsy Maltese greeting I'd heard the locals use and asked him the way to St. Thomas Bay. He nodded cheerfully and, without saying a word, pointed me toward a small dirt road snaking up the ridgeline.

"Thank you," I said, bowing slightly and bidding him farewell.

With a quick snap of the driver's reins they were off. I made my way up the road to a foot trail that crested on the cliffs overlooking St. Thomas Bay. I had become somewhat infatuated with Malta's gorgeous scenery and gazed down with pleasure at the morning sun reflecting off the shimmering sea. Malta's ever-present fishing boats slowly trolled up and down the shoreline, fishing for amberjack and bream that were schooling around the reef.

Unlike Marsaxlokk Bay, St. Thomas wasn't quaint, charming, or anything remotely resembling a tourist attraction. It was a simple working man's fishing village with small fishing huts and tiny homes dotting the shoreline. It did have a nice sandy beach with a rock seawall behind it, where fishermen had spread their nets to dry in the early morning sun.

In my thinking, this was one of the last prospects in my search for a bay that fit the biblical narrative. I pulled out my Bible and nautical maps and read again the account of Paul's shipwreck. Starting where around midnight the sailors initially "sensed" they were nearing land, I followed the account verse-by-verse, retracing and reviewing everything.

> Now when the fourteenth night had come...the sailors
> sensed that they were drawing near some land.
> (Acts 27:27)

I looked out into the bay. Here, as everywhere on Malta, the shoreline was broken in sections by high rock cliffs and jagged outcroppings. Yet I noticed a difference. To this point in my search, I had yet to find a place where the sailors on Paul's ship would have heard a thunderous roar of waves breaking over a reef—and breaking *before,* not after, it was too late to do anything about it. But here, stretching out and guarding the approach to St. Thomas Bay from the southeast, was the Munxar Reef—a fingerlike submerged protrusion extending a mile and a half out to sea. Judging from its size and peculiar angle from shore, it seemed to fit exactly with the narrative of Luke.

> *And they took soundings and found it to be twenty fathoms [120 feet]; and when they had gone a little farther, they took soundings again and found it to be fifteen fathoms [90 feet].* (v. 28)

Sitting down and using the bare dirt as a calculator, I spread out my navigation charts of the waters surrounding Malta, then rechecked the contour lines and recorded depths of the approach to St. Thomas Bay. Obviously depths change on the seafloor, but here the depths aligned with the 120-foot sounding, and then with the 90-foot sounding taken prior to reaching the outer edge of a reef (as found in Luke's description). All other depth readings on the west and southwest coast of Malta were abrupt, with sheer seafloor drop-offs.

I knew of those Roman ports on the northeastern coast of Malta that the sailors would have recognized. All the criteria for the correct place of the shipwreck lined up at St. Thomas Bay—and no other place—on the shoreline of Malta. St. Thomas Bay was also the one place on Malta where, as the old man told me, two seas come together. It was also the only place I'd seen where during a violent gregale the waves crashed over Munxar Reef, creating a huge wall of waves out to sea, *away* from the bay's mouth.

As I sat on the cliff overlooking St. Thomas Bay, I imagined I could see what the men aboard Paul's ship might have seen from the deck of that Alexandrian vessel over nineteen centuries ago.

Sharp-rising cliffs towered off to their left and sheer rocks threatened them to their right. An empty sea was all they saw extending in all directions away from the tiny island. Their storm-tossed nightmare had run its course; their fate seemed sealed. To challenge the malevolent sea anymore would mean destruction. Their only hope was to somehow get the ship past the crashing waves on the reef and into the protection of the bay.

Luke, the eyewitness, described it this way:

> *When it was day, they did not recognize the land; but they observed a bay with a beach, onto which they planned to run the ship if possible. (v. 39)*

Once again, Luke's formal education and his training as a medical professional allowed him to spell out perfectly the predicament in which these men found themselves. Luke's use of the phrase "if possible" in describing their chances of making it past the reef derives from a Greek phrase extremely rare in the New Testament. In Greek, the combination of words used by Luke to say "if possible"— describing the likely odds of successfully making it to the safe waters of the bay—actually indicate the "least likely" chance of completing the maneuver. Luke was saying in effect, "They observed a beach, onto which, if possible—though probably not possible—they planned to run the ship."[14] Another translation might read: "Not really a chance in the world."

So it isn't difficult to realize that whatever Luke saw from the deck of the freighter that miserable dawn sufficiently discouraged any real optimism at actually reaching the beach, much less running the ship aground there. Still, he and the others knew they would have to "go for it" to have any chance at all.

On this sunny morning, watching the lazy fishing boats trolling the pristine waters, I struggled to transport myself back in time to glimpse the sailors' gloomy prospects that morning. From where I stood, the only obstacle that could have elicited such despair was the Munxar Reef. Surely they could see the storm's massive swells smashing and rolling on the reef directly in front of them. The power of the waves breaking on that reef would cut them to ribbons. I had the advantage from shore, of course, and could see that the reef was in fact punctuated by a few breaks and deep cuts—any one of which might have allowed a much smaller, shallower craft to pass through. However, a big Alexandrian grain freighter would surely run aground on the reef. So they had no choice but to attempt to lighten the ship.

> *And as day was dawning, Paul implored them all to take food.... So when they had eaten enough, they lightened the ship and threw out the wheat into the sea.* (vv. 33a, 38)

Verse 38 says they lightened the ship by throwing out the last of the grain, which was stored loose in the belly of the ship, sacrificing ballast and stability for a shallow run at the reef.

In the chaos of the storm and realizing that the ship was sinking, it had been decided: They would make a run for the beach. To the storm-worn men standing on deck, the supreme moment had arrived. In a final desperate, last-ditch effort they would cut the anchor lines, leaving the anchors in the sea. They would point the ship at the crashing waves on the reef before them and try for the safe haven of the small harbor and sandy beach. Either they would somehow make it to shore and survive, or they would be shredded on the rocks.

THE SUPREME MOMENT

How can a person fully relate to the fear of those 276 men? A person can't, though I knew very well the feeling of dread and anticipation when facing a life-or-death moment. At one time or another, some people experience that electrified moment when they know that to proceed may well mean death. During my career as a policeman, those episodes were all too frequent.

I still vividly recall the day in Southern California, years ago, when I responded to a potentially deadly situation involving two men who had barricaded themselves in a house after shooting and wounding a girlfriend. They were angry, drunk, and desperate and were armed with a rifle and a knife. The girlfriend had run, wounded and screaming, down the street to escape. But the girl's father remained inside, held hostage at gunpoint. The men were making irrational demands and threatening to shoot the father. The more we tried to reason with them, the more irrational they became.

After fruitless negotiations, we feared that the father's life was in imminent danger. A critical moment had arrived. Two small teams of officers would storm the house. One group would enter through an open window on the side of the house; another would break down the front door and enter head-on. I was told to "volunteer" to be one of four men going through the front of the house.

Once we were in position, the police chief gave the signal, and both teams made their move to enter the home. Originally I was second in line to go through the front door, but as the officer in front of me raised his foot to kick in the door, he hesitated. It was as if his mind was telling him, "This is not the logical thing to do. If my foot extends and knocks the door off its hinges and I go in through that door, I may die." But this was not the time for us to have a philosophical discussion on the reasons why he froze at the door stoop. We had been given an order, and other officers were already climbing through a side window (one of which was my best friend Sig Swanstrom), trusting that we were entering through the door. The next moments were a blur—all I recall is my foot kicking past the officer in front of me and the door swinging out of the way.

To my great relief no shots were fired, and after a brief scuffle the suspects were subdued. When I went through the door that day, I was scared. My heart was pounding in my ears. In a way, I can appreciate the fear those on Paul's ship would have felt in that violent storm, as they sailed into the crashing waves of the reef in an attempt to somehow make it to shore.

A RUN FOR THE BEACH

On that night in the first century, staring at Munxar Reef, the men aboard Paul's ship faced their moment of truth. As they laid knife blades to the four taut braided ropes, they knew they could not turn back. Once they cut the ropes, they had sealed their own fate.

And they let go the anchors and left them in the sea. (v. 40)

Interestingly enough, the King James translation uses different terminology: "when they had *taken* up the anchors." This translation had compelled me, months earlier, to verify that the anchors had indeed been abandoned overboard. As it turns out, earlier in the same account, Luke described the men's despair such that "all hope that we would be saved was eventually given up" (v. 20). A careful study of the first century *Koine* Greek clarified this inconsistency and convinced me that the anchors were left in the sea. I learned that there was a mistranslation of the word, περιαιρεω which literally means "to take away altogether or entirely." The Greek word εαω means "to let alone, to give up, let go, or leave." After a careful review of the Greek, there could be no doubt that the ropes had been cut and the anchors left in the sea.[15]

> ...*loosing the rudder ropes; and they hoisted the main-*
> *sail to the wind and made for shore.* (v. 40)

When the crew cut the ropes, experienced crewmen, who had been prevented from escaping the ship the night before, jerked loose the slip-knots holding the two huge steering oars astern and let them drop into the churning water. As the massive ship lurched forward, freed from the grasp of the anchors, frantic sailors in the bow hoisted the one remaining foresail to the still-formidable wind. The massive freighter was only a two-master. The large main mast amidships, which was held by a wide mizzen yard, was probably down, as some translations suggest. If that was the case, the smaller sail mounted in the bow area, on the foremast, was now all they had to sail the ship.

With nothing to hold the ship back, the terrible wind pushed against the small sail, and along with the rolling waves, drove the ship ahead. Every man onboard must have braced himself, waiting for the inevitable dreadful impact with the reef submerged beneath the crashing waves directly in their path.

The freighter went headlong into the fuming wall of white water— the "place of two seas"—which was converging in a violent tempest upon the reef. The sailors knew that to pound the reef, list sideways, and capsize outside the bay would mean death for all but a lucky few. Their only real hope of survival lay in riding the storm swells through the narrow rift of the reef and somehow making it to shore. But if they would come to grief on the rocks, they would try to swim to shore, which, as it turned out, is exactly what they did.

> But striking a place where two seas met, they ran the ship aground; and the prow stuck fast and remained immovable, but the stern was being broken up by the violence of the waves. (v. 41)

The roar of wood crashing into rock resounded in a cacophony of splintering timbers, crashing waves, and screaming men. Hitting the reef with such force sent the huge bulk of the ship onto the reef, where it "stuck fast," stranding the crew at the critical, desperate threshold of safety.

The front part of the ship slid up on the reef, and the aft was submerged in the sea. The waves began to pound the ship's transom to pieces, tearing it apart as the stern gave way to the waves smashing the deck amidships. What would they do? Suddenly, the lives of 276 men became the responsibility of one man alone—the centurion Julius.

71

> *And the soldiers' plan was to kill the prisoners, lest any*
> *of them should swim away and escape.* (v. 42)

It was the kind of moment for which every Roman soldier had long trained. As with modern military units, the Roman army drilled its soldiers to respond instantly to any crisis, and the sinking of a ship at sea was no exception. In this case, however, the pride and power of the Roman state superseded a mere prisoner's safety, and as the waves ripped the ship apart and men prepared to swim for shore, a real chance existed for prisoners who survived to perhaps escape. Rome's policy of "death before escape" kicked in, and the soldiers onboard prepared to hastily execute the prisoners so they could make their *own* escape.

> *But the centurion wanted to spare Paul's life and kept*
> *them from carrying out their plan. He ordered those*
> *who could swim to jump overboard first and get to*
> *land.* (v. 43)

At the last moment, Julius stepped in and countermanded Roman law, surely recalling Paul's claim that *all* would make it safely to shore (v. 34). And according to Luke, Julius had specific designs to save Paul. Julius ordered all those who could swim, which included the soldiers, to head for shore first. He then gave the order for everyone else to abandon the doomed freighter and make for land on shattered debris—boards, beams, and broken masts—upon which the stragglers would float to shore.

Like rats escaping from a flooded bilge, the crew and prisoners groped, gasped, and slowly, one by one, pulled themselves ashore. The soft sand of that beach was a long-awaited feeling of salvation.

It must have been an incredible, unbelievable scene for the Maltese natives to awaken to that morning—the sight of a monstrous freighter breaking apart on the reef. And as they watched—perhaps from the same place I was standing—one pitiful form after another slowly creeping up the sand, their hearts must have gone out to those survivors. Waiting, watching, and running from one sea-battered survivor to the next, they probably kept count. One survivor...then ten...then fifty...then more than a hundred! To the islanders' astonishment, all 276 men had somehow made it safely to the beach.

I stared down at the nautical maps and Bible before me. The words from Luke, penned so long ago, spoke to me of a place where "two seas meet," of "Syrtis," and "Euroclydon," here on this obscure Maltese shoreline. Suddenly the biblical narrative converged and came to life in a swirl of compass headings and images, pointing me to this exact place.

In that moment, I knew what I would have to do: return to Colorado, regroup, recruit some expert divers, and return to try and find the lost anchors of Paul, which I hoped lay hidden and waiting for me under the blue waters of the Munxar Reef. ⚓

Chapter Six

THE BIG CAVE

*O*ver the next months, I began assembling a research team to join me in Malta. If I truly intended to explore the reef and seabed beneath St. Thomas Bay, I needed experienced divers. I had no idea what to expect from Malta's coastal waters, its peculiar tides and currents, and I would need people trained in undersea exploration if I had any chance of finding Paul's sea anchors. I received Jean François's name from a friend, who told me he would be the perfect teammate.

Master diver, Jean François La Archevec, hailed from Canada and was now serving as a dive superintendent based on Her Majesty's Canadian ship *York* in Toronto. My friend told me Jean François had been involved with the diving expeditions that located the *Edmund Fitzgerald*, which sank on Lake Superior in November 1975, and the downed Swiss Air Flight 111, which crashed into the sea near Halifax, Nova Scotia, in September 1998.

I called Jean François for an interview, and without hesitating he told me in his strong French-Canadian accent that he would love to dive in Malta. "It will be a welcome break from the cold waters of Canada," he said, volunteering the account of a recent brush with death he'd had in Halifax Harbor. He was in freezing waters beneath the waterline working on the steel plating of a huge ship, when the wake from a passing cruiser pushed the ship he was working on against the flat concrete dock behind him.

"I would have been crushed. I was trapped—" he said. "If I hadn't found a small space in the pier wall to crawl into... I was stuck, squeezed in like a coffin, and thought I would freeze—or my air would run out. It felt like I would be trapped forever, but after some time the ship slowly moved out a few feet and I swam out.

"Once again," he said with a weary chuckle, "I survived." His tone was that of a man who had escaped more than a few brushes with death. Jean François said he would be available to join me on my search for the sea anchors.

I had found the first member of my team.

My friend gave me the name of another Canadian who was a sailing specialist named David Laddell, who also owned a company called Sea-Ex. Laddell had both the equipment and the availability to go on our search and also readily agreed to join our team.

In the meantime, I had independently recruited Dr. Mark Phillips, a Ph.D. in religious studies, to coordinate our research efforts and act as a liaison with the international scholarly community. The addition of Dr. Phillips's wife, Angela, and friend Mitch Yellen rounded out the team I would need for the next phase of our search.

With the group set, and the logistics worked out, I began making final plans to return to Malta.

ST. THOMAS BAY

Our team arrived in Malta in September 2001 and wasted no time renting a van from the airport. Dr. Phillips, who had done his doctoral work in Oxford, England, took the wheel—the only one among us who dared attempt driving on the "wrong" side of the road (as a former British colony, Malta still employs British-style driving). Mark expertly navigated the narrow Maltese roads to Marsaxlokk Bay.

After a quick lunch, we drove to St. Thomas Bay to visit the Aqua Bubbles Diving School, a renowned divers' emporium that bustles with customers all day every day during the dive season. Walking into the shop, we passed a group of men who carried a load of empty cylinders in and clanked them down on the concrete floor. The place smelled of the sea and rubber suits, and rippled with loud conversations of divers discussing the comparative merits of their day beneath the waves: how beautifully clear the water was or what types of exotic fish swam by. A compressor in the corner hummed like a miniature jackhammer as divers swapped stories, laughed, and soaked in the contagious, fraternal atmosphere of sport diving, Maltese-style.

People dive in the sea for different reasons, but as often as not they do it to escape the cluttered, frenetic world we live in. The undersea world is silent and veritably scintillates with the vibrant colors and alien textures of the marine life it supports. The sea has an enchanting, almost seductive allure, inviting us to a world not designed for us *humans,* yet beckoning us into its unseen world of dazzling spectacle and incomparable diversity.

Since the oceans cover roughly 71 percent of the earth's surface, our planet should probably be called *Ocean* instead of *Earth*. And here among all these major bodies of water—the Pacific, Atlantic, Indian, and Arctic; the North Sea, Baltic, Bering, and Mediterranean—I had come to Malta to try to find a shipwreck that occurred two thousand years ago. What would cause me to think that I, not even a certified diver, could find a Roman-era sea anchor on the earth's 130 million square miles of seafloor? It was a foolhardy notion at best, except for the fact that I had in my possession a treasure map—*the Bible*—a document I had long ago learned should allow me to pinpoint the exact location.

TREASURE MAP

There is something intriguing about a treasure map, conjuring images and recollections of children's books and pirate movies. I still vividly remember sitting with my older brother Paul in the flickering light of a darkened movie theater, popcorn boxes wedged in our laps, watching the gruesome antics of some surly, peg-legged pirate with a patch over his eye. Of course the pirate usually had a gray beard, wore a fancy red jacket, and carried a sword and pistol in his waistband....

I can see the captain spreading a map over a big rock as blue waves lapped at the beach in the background. The old map was weathered and yellow, with a big red *X* marking the spot where the treasure lay buried. The scrawny band of pirates anxiously stood by holding shovels, leaning over the map with eager anticipation. The captain ran his finger along the dotted lines that lead to where the treasure was buried.

"Thirty paces east from the rock," he growled. "It looks like a skull on the cliff."

Carrying the map, he marked off each pace, slow and sure.

"Fifteen paces to the crossed palm trees, then ten paces to a clearing in the jungle."

As the captain pointed his finger to the spot, the pirates began to dig, faster and faster, until they heard the dull *thud* of shovel blade on wood. Usually they wrestled to the surface a box the size of a big steamer trunk, with hinges that could've been taken from a dungeon door. A huge, rusty padlock sealed the creaky clasp, and the captain, dramatically pulling his pistol from his waistband, aimed and shot. The next instant saw a quick, flashing boom and a puff of smoke, smashing the lock and flinging open the chest to reveal a glittering bundle of gold and jewels....

I love old movies about treasure and pirates.

Standing in the dive shop, I felt that same excitement of seeking lost treasure. I had no doubt that every diver who had ever visited this busy shop held out hope of one day scanning the seafloor and eyeing some half-buried amphora jar, or a barnacle-encrusted coin, or even the heart-stopping glint of a gold doubloon.

It was not gold *I* sought, but lead: four lead anchors lying on the ocean floor in ninety feet of water near a bay with a beach where *two seas meet* on the southeast coast of Malta. With my maps, ocean guides, and nautical instruments, I had, in concentric circles, narrowed the possibilities down to one small patch of seafloor. Now, with my fully equipped dive team, I would have to cover the final distance from the sea's surface to the seabed.

While we waited our turn to query a member of the shop's dive staff, a big man with a dark Mediterranean look walked into the room. Everyone turned, smiled, and met him fondly with shouts of *"Hey, Ray!"* This was obviously a man all the divers looked up to—the owner of the shop, but something even more than that. The near unanimous outflow of affection and respect told me that this man was almost a father figure to these people.

I worked my way through the crowd and approached Ray. As he glanced my way, I shouted above the noise, "Excuse me, I'd like to ask you a question."

"What?" Ray yelled back, distracted by the bedlam around him. "Are you interested in diving?"

"Not exactly," I replied, trying to be discreet in this pack of experienced divers. "I *do* want to ask you a question."

"What." Ray quickly answered back in the clipped manner of a man accustomed to getting straight to the point.

Leaning forward I said, "It's about a shipwreck. An ancient shipwreck."

Ray stopped and stared at me for a moment, then said, with arched brow, "A *shipwreck?* I think we should go outside."

As Ray, Jean François, and I worked our way toward the door, I looked quickly around and was relieved that no one seemed interested in following. Just outside the front door, a handful of divers and employees busied themselves with washing down wetsuits and dive gear in huge tubs of fresh water. We stopped a few paces away, and I stared out at St. Thomas Bay, a ready-made visual aid for my explanation.

I introduced Jean François as "a master diver from Canada" and softly added, "My name is Bob Cornuke. I am trying to find the location of an ancient lost shipwreck."

Ray didn't mince words. "How old is this shipwreck?"

"It happened over one thousand nine hundred years ago," I said.

"Ah…from olden times?"

"Yes," I said, with a deferring nod.

"From Roman times?"

I again nodded yes.

"Well, you won't find any wreck from that long ago." He sniffed. "The wood's all been eaten up by organisms in the water."

"I know that," I said politely. "But I think maybe something from the ship may have lasted all these years."

Instinctively, Ray turned to look at the blue water of the bay, which was now churning into whitecaps because of the late afternoon wind outside the bay.

He turned to me and said matter-of-factly, "Are you speaking about anchors? Big Roman anchors?"

"Yes," I said, startled that he had anticipated the exact objects of our search. "Yes...I believe we can find the anchors from Paul's shipwreck."

"So you want to dive in St. Paul's Bay?" he asked.

"No," I replied. "I don't believe Paul's shipwreck was in St. Paul's Bay."

"Well, I don't think you'd find them there anyway," Ray said with a shrug. "That area's been searched pretty good, and they've found no 'Paul's shipwreck' yet."

I decided to end the secrecy of my search and told Ray of my findings, from start to finish. Beginning with my own shipwreck in Ethiopia, I explained my theory about Paul's ill-fated route to Malta and the Roman freighter's tortured, wind-blown course from Crete down toward the coast of Libya, then up to the southeast corner of Malta to the corner of the island where we now stood. I explained my thoughts about the bay with a beach and suggested that St. Thomas Bay, directly before us, wouldn't have been easily recognized by the sailors on Paul's ship. I then told Ray about my opinion on the phrase "where two seas meet" and how it perfectly fit the tide profile of St. Thomas Bay and how the ship of Paul ran aground on the reef before breaking to pieces in the waves.

At this point, Ray referred back to the two seas. "Bob, describe again the two seas. What does that mean?"

In a matter of minutes, Ray had become deeply intrigued by my theory. I took a Bible out of my backpack and read him the description from Acts 27. I then explained that the Greek word τοπος διθλασσος literally means a tongue of land, the extremity of which is covered by waves, or a projecting reef or bar against which the waves dash on both sides.[16]

He reflected on the passage for a moment before excitedly interjecting, "Right here in front of us, on the Munxar Reef, the currents come together during a storm. I have seen it many times. A huge wall of water—a white, foamy mass of colliding waves—extends almost a mile and a half out into the ocean from the mouth of the bay. It looks like a huge white snake crawling across the water."

He stood rubbing his forehead, as if finally understanding a Bible passage he had certainly read, and reread. "It is unmistakable," he added. "This really *would* be where the two seas meet. In a storm, that is exactly what it looks like."

I took this immediate response from perhaps the island's preeminent diver as great encouragement. Next I showed Ray where the Bible describes how the sailors cut loose the anchors after a ninety-foot sounding. He sat down on a large boulder outside his dive shop. Looking out to sea, he said nothing for several seconds. Then he looked back at me and said—so slowly and softly that I could barely make out the word—*"Tony."*

"I'm sorry," I said. "What was that?"

"Tony…" With obvious affection he began to share: "When I was a young boy, I knew a man named Tony. He was a powerful man and an amazing athlete. Everyone on the island knew of Tony. He held records in shot put, discus, and javelin. He was also a diving fanatic. Whether at a party, wedding, or gathering of any kind, all Tony talked about was spearfishing and diving.

He paused and said sadly, "He died in the sea. His body was missing for seven years. Then one day he was found in a cave. He was still in his wetsuit. His speargun was by his side."

I could see that it was a memory almost too painful to bear, but Ray continued, "Well, Bob," he said, pointing lazily toward the bay. "When I was fourteen years old, Tony and I saw anchors out there. They were anchors from olden times, probably Roman. We brought up two. We later heard rumors from others that two more were brought up from the same spot."

It took me a moment to grasp what I had just heard. *"Four anchors…*from the same spot?"

"Yes," Ray said, "but I never even thought these anchors could possibly be from Paul's shipwreck. After all, this is not St. Paul's Bay. This is not supposed to be the spot. But if what you're telling me is true, these anchors may be from that ship."

With a heavy sigh, Ray said under his breath, "Leave it up to Tony to find Paul's anchors." Ray paused and thought about this for a few moments. "I think he would be proud. Yes, I think he would be happy."

I waited for a moment or two, then asked, "Can you take me to the spot? The spot where you found the anchors?"

"Yes—that will be easy."

"How will you know the spot?"

"That's simple," Ray continued. "It's the area Tony called 'The Bank,' a place where we could always find the big grouper and make a little money. The day we found the anchors, they lay in the sand in front of a big cave. We would always swim down through the top of a huge crack in the rock, and it would bring us out into an enormous cave. You could put twenty school buses inside this cave. So you can see that it would be hard for me to forget. When we found the anchors, we were in front of the big cave."

"How deep is the water?" I asked.

"I don't know. Maybe twenty, twenty-five, thirty meters or so. But I can take you there. I'll take you to the big cave."

Jean François, who had been listening intently, grinned quietly, elated to hear such optimistic news. He and I planned to meet Ray at the dock the following morning and take a boat out to Munxar Reef—to "The Bank"—and dive to the big cave where the large groupers swim. ⚓

Chapter Seven

FIFTEEN FATHOMS

*E*veryone we passed the next morning on our way to the dock
called out, "Hey, Ray!" or "Hey, Ciancio!"—the nickname given
by Tony when Ray was a young boy. Clearly something of Tony's legendary
popularity on Malta had been passed on to Ray, who carried the mantle of
island diving-icon proudly—and well.

The morning air felt warm and calm as we arrived at the dock and waited for the rest of our team to arrive. The sea was quiet and the sky clear. We planned to go out to the area of the big cave where Ray said as a young man he and Tony had found anchors. I tried to simply accept Ray's claim at face value, though many questions still hung in the air. Questions such as, why had Ray so far refused to volunteer any hint of the anchors' whereabouts? Part of me yearned to ask him outright, but I didn't press it at this point. I could tell by Ray's manner—friendly, yet protectively aloof—that we hadn't yet established a rapport necessary for me to cross that line.

Something else not altogether unexpected had occurred to me. I could sense, in Ray's guarded words and mildly standoffish body language, something distinctly mysterious, even *taboo,* about the whole affair of the sea anchors. It put me on guard and alerted me to be extra conscious of the island's unspoken code. I could easily sabotage the entire exploration if I asked the wrong question at the wrong moment. As such, I kept my expectations in check. I wouldn't ask Ray for specifics until I knew for certain the timing was right. For now, he seemed willing to take us to the reef and show us around, and that would have to suffice.

I planned to go out to the reef and let Jean François, David Laddell, and a Maltese diver from Ray's shop take independent measurements of the seafloor. The idea was to determine how deep the water was where they had supposedly, almost three decades earlier, discovered anchors. If the depth held consistent with Luke's eyewitness account—"And they took soundings and found it to be twenty fathoms (120 feet); and when they had gone a little farther, they took soundings again and found it to be fifteen fathoms (90 feet)" (Acts 27:28)—I could count it a significant clue.

My calculations from nautical maps put the anchors' drop zone at ninety feet at the outside Munxar Reef area, close to the outer marker buoy. Would Ray's big cave, the area of Tony's Bank, also be located at that spot?

Jean François and the rest of our team finally came sauntering down the pier, and we began loading Ray's boat with an array of sophisticated diving gear—sleek cylinders, shiny regulators, buoyancy compensators, fins, masks, wet suits, weight belts. Admiring this gleaming stockpile, I couldn't help but think how the sport of diving has changed so much in such a short period of time. Early divers in the Mediterranean used flight goggles layered with putty, helmets that leaked or broke apart under pressure, and pressurized tanks with unreliable nonautomatic air regulators. For those adventurous first divers, even routine dives were a death-defying risk.

But with quantum advances in Aqua-Lung, or scuba (Self Contained Underwater Breathing Apparatus), technology in the 1940s and 1950s, everything changed. Once scuba technology arrived on the scene, it didn't take long for serious diving to become a popular sport and a borderline flamboyant, avant-garde lifestyle on Malta. By the early 1960s, a tight-knit fraternity of local divers had begun to make a name for themselves on Malta—much as extreme skiing had once spilled out of the Rockies, or dirt bike clubs arose in the Mojave Desert—revolving around the cult-of-personality energy of island *celebrities* like Tony and, later, Ray.

These lithe, lean-muscled jocks, chased ever-greater depths and probed increasingly inaccessible, secret fishing lairs and remote reefs. The boy Ray simply counted himself the eager young protégé of the man named Tony; together they chased after the big fish that brought fast cash at the local restaurants.

I marveled as I listened to Ray spin through his memory reel of those early Maltese divers—who relied on crude equipment, and according to Ray, often dived without even consulting decompression tables. Some learned basic diving techniques and principles from a British Navy diving team stationed on the island, and others got their education word-of-mouth from other divers or from whatever reference books they could scrounge up. Consequently, most of the divers in Ray's circle simply did not know how to avoid, much less respond to, the extreme dangers associated with all but the most routine forays beneath the waves.

Ray recalled that several of his friends tragically perished because they did not even realize that they had limited time underwater; they stayed down too long, until their tanks were almost empty, and then suffered the deadly consequences of decompression sickness (otherwise known as the bends) from racing to the surface. Fortunately, many lives were probably saved because most of those divers did not have wetsuits and simply got too cold to stay down long or swim too deep to get into serious trouble. Still, to hear Ray describe it, the death rate had been high.

As technology improved, however, those same divers were the first to strap on modern Aqua-Lungs and penetrate the unsearched depths off the coast of Malta. In doing so, young boys and novice divers alike routinely came across rare, ancient artifacts long lost to the sea and hidden from history for hundreds, even thousands, of years. It was a secret, brash society of amateur treasure hunters, whose members may or may not have understood that, in many cases, the artifacts they stumbled upon had vast historical significance. Sadly, most of these early reef explorers had little regard for the value of these ancient artifacts and did nothing to protect, much less preserve, the rich archeological trove uncovered in those early days of Maltese scuba diving.

Listening as Ray described those early reef dives, I could only wonder, with some misgiving, at the fate of the anchors.

Today, of course, it's a different story. To ensure high standards of safety as well as the protection of natural, historical, and archaeological resources, the government carefully monitors all diving on Malta. Spearfishing, for one, is absolutely forbidden, and all archaeological finds must be reported immediately; some areas of the island are off-limits to divers altogether, and all divers are required to meet international licensing requirements and guidelines. Anyone who straps on an oxygen tank must present a medical certificate, passport photograph, and logbook before receiving a dive permit.

Ray confessed to being a rare living bridge between diving as it was "back then" and diving today. As one of the first to probe the deep waters of Malta, Ray rose to become the technical officer of the Federation of the Underwater Activities of Malta and is a current CMAS instructor. Yet, unlike in his carefree youth, Ray now carefully monitors diving activities on the island and helps enforce the rigid requirements set down by the Maltese government to protect the safety of other divers and the cultural heritage of his native island.

Hearing Ray talk about the old days, I couldn't believe what seemed to me to be an incredible contrast—standing on a boat loaded down with some of the best technology our modern world has to offer and using it to locate artifacts spoken of in the ancient text of the Bible. Standing in the warming morning breeze, I wondered if Luke, in writing the words, "and casting off the anchors, they left them in the sea," had ever, for even an instant, imagined anyone finding them.

Luke wrote more words about the voyage and shipwreck of Paul than were included in the entire creation account in Genesis. His detailed narrative was now coming to life for me as we climbed aboard Ray's boat and cast off the lines. Ray said, "Ready?" and in an almost simultaneous motion cranked the engine to life and slammed the throttle forward, jolting us back as the big brass propellers bit into the sea. Within five minutes we were circling over the dive site on Munxar Reef, peering over the side into the crystalline, glass-smooth water. Ray carefully leaned over the side, scanning the seabed, searching for familiar landmarks. All I could make out was the great, dark mass of the reef. Suddenly, Ray turned off the engine and grabbed an iron anchor attached to a long coiled chain. He casually tossed it over the side, and we waited as the chain rattled to a jerking stop a few seconds later.

"This is it," Ray said, securing the anchor chain. "We're over the big cave."

I looked at my charts, the outer marker buoy, the shoreline, the outline of the reef below our boat, and my pulse quickened. We were floating directly over the spot on the reef where I had calculated the sailors on Paul's ship had dropped the four anchors!

The dive crew slipped on their short summer wetsuits and busied themselves with the careful ritual of readying their gear—turning on the air, checking and double-checking the regulators and gauges. With the smoothness of hundreds of repetitions, they donned vests, weight belts, fins, and masks as naturally as children dressing for school. Soon they were sitting side by side on the gunwales, waiting for Ray's signal. With a thumbs-up from Ray, they leaned backward and splashed into the sea. Quickly righting themselves on the surface, they cleared their masks, gave an OK sign to Ray, and rolled forward, finning downward to disappear into a swirl of bubbles.

Ray led their slow descent to the area where he said they had found the anchors. They cruised down in front of the big cave opening, then swam out onto a sandy stretch of seafloor where tufts of sea grass swayed in the gentle current. Settled on the bottom of the seafloor, Jean François unlashed a depth indicator attached to a lanyard on his arm. Carefully reading the gauge, he looked up at Ray and flashed another OK sign. Nodding in approval, Ray pointed up and the four started their slow ascent to the surface. The whole transaction took but a few moments— they had taken the depth reading and paddled back upward.

Popping through the surface, Jean François removed the regulator from his mouth, looked up at me with a grin and said, "The place where the guide showed us…it registered about ninety feet on the bottom."

Ninety feet. I stared back down at the reef, it's dark form lying motionless below. My mind instinctively traced back through the steps of the biblical narrative and replayed the sequence of Paul's shipwreck. From directly above the dive site, I could easily see that in a storm the sea would gather and converge into a fierce wall of water on the long strand of reef. I turned to scan the shoreline. High white cliffs framed the harbor to its left, and on the other side of the narrow island nothing but jagged cliffs terminating into an open sea. If they had anchored at this spot, they would have no option but to try for shore and the protection of St. Thomas Bay. Everything seemed to fit—and now, even the depth of the sea fit. In geographic synchronization, the location below me converged precisely with the words printed on the pages of the Bible.

That was the moment when, in my mind, everything neatly fell into place.

That moment marked the first time I actually *believed* we were floating over the exact spot of the fateful shipwreck! Exhilaration like I hadn't felt in years washed over me, and with it countless unanswered questions: *Where was the anchor Ray and Tony had apparently found? Would Ray ever tell me, or would I have to look elsewhere for answers? And what of the* other *anchors? Did they still lie somewhere below, buried in the sand, or had some other diver found* them *as well?* These questions would have to be answered. I would never be able to validate my theory of Paul's shipwreck without some hard evidence of the anchors themselves.

Jean François, Ray, and the other divers tossed their fins and gear in the boat, and I helped them climb back onboard. I stayed quiet, certain now that all of the research I'd done, all the interviews, expense, and travel, had led me to this electric moment in time. I'd had my suspicions about this side of the island, but now, for the first time, I knew I'd latched on to the true scent of this historic quarry.

The first leg of my journey seemed complete. But with this flush of excitement came an equally potent pang of anxiety. Headed back toward Ray's shop, skimming across the waters of St. Thomas Bay in the boat, I felt the familiar tug of realization that my real work on Malta had only just begun. ⚓

Chapter Eight

REMEMBERING TONY

I helped Jean François, Dave, and the Maltese diver place their gear in mesh duffel bags, which we carried up the pathway to the Aqua Bubbles Diving School. A young boy waiting at the dock carried Ray's gear as if he were his personal butler. I could see in the boy's upward glances and body language the admiration he had for Ray.

We paused for a moment at a shaded lean-to to get out of the sun. It was hot. Ray was red-faced and sweating in his wetsuit, yet seemed in no hurry to leave the water's edge. There are men who can never leave the ocean to live in the mountains or the desert. For these natural-born mariners, life itself lies in the smell of the sea and the sound of the waves. That was Ray.

He sat down on a wooden bench, wet suit and all, letting us know without speaking that it wasn't time to leave. Perhaps now would be a good time to ask him more specifically about the anchor.

"Would you mind telling me in more detail of Tony and the anchors from the Munxar?" I asked.

"Where do you want me to start?"

"Start with Tony if you could," I said. "How did you come to know him?"

"Well, Bob," he began, speaking softly, "Tony gave me the nickname of 'Ciancio' when I was just thirteen years old, when I started working for him. Well not working for him, but sort of just helping around the dive shop. I serviced dive equipment, painted cylinders. Every now and again—to thank me—Tony would take me on a dive.

"Yes, he was a father figure," Ray added, smiling, "always steering me in the right direction, keeping me from bad friends."

Though soft-spoken, Ray had suddenly become quite animated. I saw that he loved talking about Tony. Being out on the Munxar that day, where they had once spearfished together, had clearly dialed up a mountain of emotion. Ray's tongue had definitely loosened.

"My father left when I was very young, so Tony became...truly, my *dad*. Tony and his wife, Margaret, sort of adopted me. Many nights I would sit in their living room and listen to Tony tell dive stories, about the sea and spearing the big ones.

Ray described Tony as a super athlete, "very powerful, with broad shoulders, and stocky. He was also kind of hairy." He chuckled then, rubbing the top of his head. "Tony had no hair on the top of his head; he lost his hair very young."

Ray said that in spite of his strength, Tony was the gentlest of men, "a man who would rather discuss things than use his fists and strength." Ray paused often during his recollections, reflecting on his friend's unique character, his gentle power. "No one challenged Tony," Ray said with pride. "No one *needed* to."

To hear Ray describe him, Tony struck me as a good man, very generous, teaching the locals and tourists alike how to dive—often for free.

"The other divers would tell him, 'Tony, you're never going to make money like this.'" Ray shrugged and turned to watch the young boy carefully hosing down his cylinders. "I guess I kind of do the same thing today. I got that from Tony."

"Anyway," he concluded happily, "that's how it was with us. I would lug the cylinders to the boat; and when the cylinders were empty, I would fill them from the compressor. I would do whatever needed to be done, fix wet suits, whatever."

Ray shouted out a gentle instruction to the boy. In his approving eyes, I could see that he had installed himself as the lad's mentor, the way Tony had for him. I began to stand up, thinking we might finish the story back at the dive shop, out of the heat, but Ray didn't budge. His memory reel was rolling, and he would finish his story right where he sat.

"The first time Tony took me out to sea, I waited in the boat for him and his dive buddies to surface. But I got a little too excited. I thought, *I'm sure I can dive. I'll go down and have a look and see what Tony and his friends are doing.* Tony always had spare gear on the boat, so I just grabbed a big twinset of cylinders and put on Tony's spare weight belt, which had ten kilos on it." Ray laughed, patting his growing midsection. "I was a little scrawny guy then. I probably needed only something like *four* kilos.

"Well, I threw the cylinders on my back and strapped on that heavy weight belt. I was so heavy I should have made a hole in the boat—and I didn't have fins. I didn't have anything but the weights, the tanks, and the regulator. I went down to the bottom like a rock. Not knowing any different, I thought, *Hey, this is normal.* So I started walking on the seabed.

"Tony swam over, grabbed me, and dragged me up to the surface. He

95

probably saved me that day. I was so laden down with lead that I doubt I could've swam back to the surface." He shook his head. "Kind of a stupid thing to do, jumping over the side of the boat with so much weight strapped on me. But I was a kid and, well, that was the way of it in those early days."

As for the sport of spearfishing, Ray said Tony had always ranked as Malta's best, hands down. He won almost every competition held on the island to test technique and accuracy and (true to form, I thought) even occasionally dropped out to give the other divers a chance.

"Tony taught me to shoot a speargun," Ray recalled, "but I was sort of impatient." He raised his arms in the firing position. "I sometimes fired my spear too quick, so…I missed a lot."

Whereas he recalled Tony's memory with true reverence, he described his spearfishing exploits with unabashed merriment. "I remember one time I shot a big grouper in the tail—a bad shot, the *worst* place you can hit a large fish," he said. "It was such a big fish, I thought, how could I miss?"

The injured fish took him for a ride, plowing through the water, leaving a small trail of blood while towing skinny young Ray along like a plastic bobber. "I was no longer a hunter, but a passenger hanging on for dear life. I let go and the spear, the line, and the fish disappeared into the darkness of a small cave."

Injured groupers, it seems, have a special defense mechanism. When a grouper swims into a rock outcropping or a crevasse in the reef, it makes itself thick, wedging its body in the rock by opening its gills. When that happens, it's almost impossible to pull it out by the tail. But for Tony it was a simple procedure.

"He swam past me, entered the cave, slid his bare hand inside the grouper's gills, and yanked it out."

Ray's voice trailed off. He stared at the ground and kicked sand at a small crab that was inching toward him. The high noon sun sparkled across the vast dark sea. Staring off at the distant horizon, Ray recalled the day he heard that Tony was missing.

"I got the call December 17, 1978. It was too horrible to describe. Everybody who knew Tony *loved* him," he continued. "The news spread across the island like wildfire. Night had come, and Tony had not returned from a day of diving alone. Most of his friends—his diving buddies—all rushed to the spot where he was last seen, but it was too late to dive, and no one was organized. There were no local diving teams to help in the search. It would be his friends—his friends would need to find him."

Ray's eyes were wide now, and I could see that in his mind, he was no longer sitting beside me. He was back in 1978.

"The rescue volunteers waited throughout the night and the early morning. The next morning all of them met at Tony's dive shop in Cresta Quay. It was painful to watch Tony's wife, Margaret, and his children endure it all. People came from all over Malta and registered their names as volunteers. They decided on grid searches—some were even drug behind boats as they peered down into the water—but no sign of Tony was found. That went on for a whole month—*nothing.*" His voice registered mild disgust at the searchers' apparent futility. "Over a hundred people participated in the search, and then they had to give up. It was as if the sea had swallowed Tony."

I sat there in the sweltering heat, utterly transfixed. Tony had been to Ray as Jim Irwin had been to me, introducing him to new worlds, launching him into his life's passion—and then, suddenly, gone. I could feel Ray's heartache, even twenty-five years later.

Seven years passed, he said, and any hope of ever finding a trace of Tony had long since disappeared. Then, in 1985, a young English diver named Chris Chapman, along with a man named Marco Briffa, took a dive on Zonqor Reef. They loved to fish and followed a large grouper into one of the caves beneath the reef. Once inside the cave, Chris angled up into a chamber that opened into a black cavernous hole in the rock.

"No one had gone that far into the cave," Ray said, "because it looked like it ended. But Chris saw the grouper go up, so he followed it. He saw a gap that went farther up and opened into another small cave. This fellow was very slow and careful," he added, explaining that many divers have perished in the caves of Malta from simply moving too fast and carelessly. Without realizing the danger, they stir up the silt and instantly become disoriented. They swim around blindly, unable to find their way, and finally their air runs out.

Ray paused for a few seconds before continuing. "As Chris moved into the hidden cave, he saw another diver. Later, he told me that he instinctively thought, *Oh look, there's Tony,* as if nothing had ever happened. But then he remembered that Tony was dead. Ray's eyes grew narrow. "But, of course, it *was* Tony. That was the cave where Tony had died—and he was there, lying flat on his face, still in his black wetsuit, gray cylinders with a red cylinder boot, his fins on, everything still as it had been the day he died."

Once Chapman realized what he was looking at, he shot out of the cave and the pair swam to the surface, understandably quite upset. After collecting themselves, they returned to shore and reported it to the authorities. Tony's body would need to be recovered. But this time his close friends couldn't do it. It was too much for them. Another team went into the cave and retrieved Tony.

Ray's eyes were now fixed on the ground. He described his painful memories as though he were watching a movie. "When they recovered Tony from the cave, they found that sand had replaced his body. Only his form had remained intact inside the wetsuit. They knew it was Tony by the watch he was wearing. It was the same watch his wife possesses, and—" he held out his wrist to show me—"the same watch I have."

Ray's words had become forced and slow. I suggested that we take a break; perhaps continue talking about this painful episode another time. Ray shook me off, and with a deep breath, said, "It's okay, Bob. I would like to tell you the rest of the story of Tony's anchors now." ⚓

Chapter Nine

TONY'S ANCHORS

*T*he young boy who had been cleaning Ray's equipment ran up to the dive shop and brought a T-shirt out to Ray. Finally feeling the effects of the sun, Ray peeled off his wet suit and, drenched in sweat, slid the gray T-shirt on.

"Thank you," he said to the boy. "That's better in this heat." Ray watched the lad walk back toward the shop and then continued reminiscing.

"I'll never forget the day we found the first anchor, Bob. We had followed the big crack at the end of Munxar and finned our way through the cave, scanning the walls for grouper. I was getting a bit experienced by now, and Tony was letting me swim close by him."

Early on in his apprenticeship to Tony, Ray had been relegated to swimming some distance behind the others out of concern that in his inexperience he might move too fast and scare the big fish away. He said Tony taught him to swim slowly, looking ahead at all times, gliding through the water unnoticed.

They had been hunting grouper the morning they found the anchor, and Ray recalled Tony setting his sights on a big one. "Tony saw a fish, then shot and missed," he said, pausing. "It was unlike Tony. I knew he would be angry about missing such a big one. He went swimming off to find the spear, stopped on the bottom, and then surprised me. He turned and waved me over, pointing down to an object that sat half beneath the sand, nearly hidden by the grass swirling around on the seafloor. I swam down and watched as Tony scraped his knife across the object. We could see right away that it was metal."

It was a huge anchor stock. From its size alone the men knew it hadn't come from a small merchant vessel or a fishing vessel, but had to have serviced on some kind of large ship.

"What we found was the stock of the anchor," he said, "the metal crosspiece. The wood and the other parts of the anchor had rotted away. All that was left was this huge piece of lead, about three, maybe four feet, long. We could see that a large section of the anchor had been cut off."

"Cut off?"

"Yes. It was cut somehow. It was half of a big anchor stock."

Ray had perked up again. Gone for now were thoughts of Tony's death. He beamed as he talked about this moment of youthful discovery with his boyhood idol. "When we surfaced after finding the anchor, Tony said that he would go for help because the anchor was so heavy. He wanted to immediately bring the anchor up from the sea. He returned with a friend, Charlie Vella, who was an instructor from his dive shop."

Ray explained that on Malta when someone finds something like an ancient anchor, or any other archaeological treasure, it is always kept within one's inner circle, within one's group—"the guys you can really trust." They put two forty-five-gallon barrels with rings welded around the openings into the boat, then headed back out to the reef. They planned to use the drums as a lifting device.[17] "But," Ray recalled, "I knew enough to realize that it wasn't going to be easy."

Back out over the reef, they tied ropes to the barrels and suited up. Ray minded the boat while Tony and Charlie dumped the barrels overboard, and then he followed them into the water. The divers let the barrels fill with water and sink to the bottom, where the trio wrestled them over to the huge piece of lead. I had assumed they wanted the anchor for its archaeological value; perhaps a reward went to those who recovered such antiquities. But then Ray told me the real reason they went to such trouble.

"To us divers, that lead was like gold," he explained. "But not for money—we used it for diving weights."

"Diving weights?" I asked, shocked.

"Yes," he said, matter-of-factly. "The anchor was cut in half and was no good to any museum—or so we thought. In those days it was very expensive to buy diving weights, and we didn't have much money. Diving weights were always sliding off divers' belts and getting lost, so there was a constant need for more. We would make our own by melting down any scavenged lead we could find and pour it into molds. But even the lead was hard to come by, so this huge, three-foot-long hunk of lead was, to us, extremely valuable."

I was stunned to hear that this historic relic, an anchor stock perhaps from the very shipwreck detailed by Luke in the book of Acts, had been used for scrap metal.

Ray continued with his tale, describing how long it took the three of them to tie the anchor stock to the barrels and then to fill the barrels with air from their cylinders. Finally, as the barrels gained buoyancy and began to rise toward the surface, the lines to the anchor tightened and, very slowly, began to budge and loosen it from the vacuum grip of the sand.

"Of course," Ray explained, "the stock was so heavy it didn't go all the way to the surface." Tony and Charlie agreed that the best thing to do was to tow the whole unstable, awkward contraption into shallower water. Eventually they managed to haul the anchor onboard and hide it in the protection of a cove.

"It took all our combined strength to heft it into the boat. All of us were straining to get that huge block of lead out of the water. It makes my back hurt again just thinking about it. But with one last heave we got it into the boat."

They took the anchor stock back to Tony's dive shop at Cresta Quay, where they cut it up into smaller pieces and melted it down to make dive weights. From the sound of it, they had quite a smelting operation going that day.

"We took the anchor and used a hacksaw to cut off sizeable chunks." Ray described how the hacksaw blades kept breaking. "Finally we began chopping the lead with chisels and used gas-fed burners to melt the lead in heavy cast-iron pots." Once a pot was full of the silvery lead soup, they poured it into a mold and left it to solidify until it could be popped out.

"We were not used to making so many weights at once," he said, "but we liked the look of all the shiny new weights lying out on the floor of the shop to cool."

"I hurried out and bought a small chisel and chiseled Tony's initials— *TM*—into the mold," Ray added. Apparently they marked each molded weight so that if any were lost and later found, they could be claimed as part of Tony's batch.

Then, as if suddenly grasping the absurdity of it all, Ray chuckled and confessed, somewhat embarrassed, "In those days we didn't look upon an object as being so valuable historically. We were young and naïve. Now I walk through museums and appreciate my heritage as a Maltese, and I cringe to think about how senseless we were. This object should have been preserved for its archaeological significance. Instead it went from being a priceless artifact to crude dive weights worth a few dollars each."

As I sat staring at him in silence, Ray caught my eye and quickly added, perhaps in self-defense, "Fortunately, we wouldn't make that same mistake again."

Anchor Number Two

Ray had already alluded to the second anchor they discovered later on the Munxar Reef. Since he knew I would want to know more about it, he continued without pausing. As I had come to expect, almost every detail of Ray's narrative had Tony as its primary centerpiece. I kept reminding myself that his memories of his old diving buddy remained far more valuable to him than the anchors I sought. And, as with almost any seafaring tale in Malta, the saga of the second anchor began with one of their spearfishing junkets.

"By now we knew to keep our eyes open while we were diving for grouper," Ray said, "just in case there were any more anchors to be found on the Munxar. We didn't really expect to find another one though, since we had been there so many times and had just happened upon the first. But still, after the first anchor, I think our eyes were a little more trained to spot something unusual."

They went out again that day to the Munxar, to "Tony's Bank," where finding a fish to kill was like money in the bank.

"To get to the Bank, we again had to go through the crack in the reef and into the cave. We came out the other side on our way to the same rock where we had found the first anchor, only a short distance from the cave. Anyway, we came out of the cave and were swimming toward the rock, and we both looked down and saw another anchor. It was a large anchor stock, not cut in half like the first, and was very close to where we had found the other one. We knew what it was right away from comparing it to the first one, so we stopped what we were doing and went straight down to it.

"Again we scraped it, and again it showed metal—lead. So we went back to the boat and agreed that we would come back, bring up the anchor, and tow it to Cresta Quay."

Ray described a slightly different strategy for landing this anchor, given the fact that this one was much heavier than the first (it hadn't been cut in half). They would bring it to the surface with the barrels like before, and then, rather than try to pull it into the boat, they would attempt to tow it behind the boat all the way to shore. They had almost broken their backs hoisting the first one into the boat and had learned their lesson.

"The day we returned for the anchor, the sea was as smooth as glass on our way out. We wouldn't have any trouble locating it because we knew that place like the back of our hands. Two other men were with us—Joe Navarro and I think a chap named David Inglott—so I would mind the boat while they dove down to the anchor and brought it up with the forty-five-gallon drums—like before. I remember that day very distinctly, because while I was topside minding the boat, the sea really began to pick up.

"You must remember," he reminded me, "I was very young and skinny as anything. There I was tending the boat when this strong cold storm blew in, whipping up big waves and dropping the temperature. After a while I was desperately cold, but I couldn't leave the divers below me. I had no choice but to sit there in the boat and…wait."

Dressed lightly and ill-prepared for bad weather, Ray soon found himself fighting hypothermia. By the time the barrels popped up to the surface with the anchor underneath them, he was shivering and blue in the cold, wet wind.

"With some difficulty I picked up the divers, but once they got onboard, they could see that I was shaking uncontrollably. Tony took off his wetsuit—which could have fit around three or four of me—and wrapped it around me. Then we started trying to tow the huge anchor against the rolling sea."

Ray told me that their twenty-one-foot boat was called the "Bathtub" and had only an old eighteen-horsepower Johnson outboard for power. Straining against the wind and storm, trying to carry the group of men and drag an anchor, the sluggish, blunt-nosed craft could hardly navigate the churning tides.

"Eventually, we decided to let the storm blow us toward the shelter of a jut of land until the wind let up," he said. "Well, unknown to us, Tony's wife, Margaret, had seen the storm moving in and had sent the Malta Coast Guard out to Munxar Reef to find us. So while we fought the anchor, the wind, and the waves, there came the Coast Guard."

Here the story took a bizarre twist. Ray said that they were afraid of the authorities after their earlier act of vandalism against the first anchor. Now, having *another* piece of archaeological contraband, instead of waving the Coast Guard in to help them, they put in behind some rocks where they couldn't be seen. With barrels in tow behind them, they knew that the possibility remained of being arrested for stealing ancient Maltese historical treasures.

"After a while the Coast Guard gave up and left," he said, seeming greatly relieved even three decades after the fact. "The storm blew over as quickly as it came. So we thought we really had it made. The sea calmed down and we started tugging the cumbersome anchor back to Cresta Quay—which took forever with that huge weight behind us."

What awaited them on shore, however, was the last thing they expected.

"When we got to Cresta Quay, there were police cars *everywhere!*" He raised his hands in amazement. "We figured we were really in trouble then, because we knew it was illegal to take old things—artifacts—out of the ocean. So we panicked, jumped into the water, and started cutting the lines holding the barrels and the anchor. We finally got it cut loose out at a point jutting out from shore and then headed in without our treasure, unsure what we would tell the police."

The surprise, of course, was on Ray, Tony, and their cohorts. They soon learned that Tony's wife had called the Coast Guard in the first place and that when they returned with no sign of Tony's boat, she thought they had sunk and probably drowned. So she called the police. It sounded like something from a Keystone Cops comedy, and Ray knew it. He couldn't help smiling while recounting that near-disaster.

"Everyone kept telling us how glad they were that we were alive and that we hadn't gone down. All we wanted to do was go back out and get our anchor. Eventually the police left and we were able to go out to where it had been 'lost' for the second time, hook it back up to the barrels, fill them with air, and tow it in the rest of the way."

Trouble seemed to haunt every stage of this clandestine salvage mission. At one point in their last-ditch effort to retrieve the anchor, the strain of the barrels broke one of the cleats loose from the back of the boat. Tony pulled Ray out of harm's way in the last split second.

"To this day, every time I look at that boat—" Ray nodded toward the dock—"and see that the cleats on the back don't match, I think about Tony and the way we brought that second anchor in from the sea."

We sat in silence for several minutes until I realized that Ray had finished his story. He had invited me into perhaps the most intimate chapter of his life, and now he seemed drained.

So that was it.

Two anchors had been found beneath those waves, deposited somehow from some ancient ship on the southeast side of the Maltese coastline. And, somehow, I found myself sitting next to perhaps the only man on Malta who would have ever known about it!

I knew I had to keep pressing forward. Doors had swung open, and I had to keep stepping through them. I now had some very important questions for Ray, questions that could define the remainder of the search effort: *What exactly did the anchor* look *like? Did it fit with the description of a Roman/Alexandrian anchor from the time of Paul?*

When I asked the first question, Ray said simply, "I'm not an expert. I don't know what year the anchor came from. It appeared to be from olden times—Roman, from what others have told me."

I knew I was treading on thin ice, but I had to ask: "Do any of the dive weights from the cut anchor that was melted down still exist?"

Ray looked at me for what seemed like the longest moment and then offered, "They may, but this was thirty years ago, and weights get lost pretty easily. Maybe some exist today, but I don't know where they would be."

"You spoke of other anchors found at this spot," I said, trying to sound casual. "Do you know if any of them exist today on the island?"

Ray sat up stiffly, looked out to sea again, and said, "The only one I know of that exists today…is the one we towed into Cresta Quay." Then he turned to me with a look that seemed to say, "That's all, no more questions!"

Chapter Ten

HOLDING HISTORY

*W*hen Ray stood up, I knew that our conversation had ended—for now. Had I penetrated too deeply into a reservoir of private information, or drawn too close to that inner circle of trust that exists among divers on Malta? The anchor Ray and Tony found had been hidden from the world's eyes for over three decades, and now I—an outsider to the island—wanted to see and photograph it.

Ray began slowly making his way up the pathway to his dive shop, squinting up at the midday sun, apparently wrestling with his thoughts—or perhaps his conscience. I walked silently alongside, aware that he had placed great trust in me within a very short amount of time. Evidence of the second anchor was important, but I knew I'd have to wait until Ray was ready.

The dive shop was alive with the usual commotion—rattling compressors, clanking cylinders, and shouted banter. I knew our conversation couldn't continue here, but just before we reached the perimeter of the shop's activity, Ray stopped, then turned around and looked at me with a seriousness I had not yet seen.

"Bob," he said, "I need to explain to you about our small group of divers, our brotherhood. We were a very close group of guys, and most of us were very young. Hotels were popping up all over Malta in the late sixties and early seventies, and the tourists all brought dollars. The hotels would charge a lot of money for meals, and the tourists were eager to pay good money to dine on our native fish. We had very special spots where we dived to get our fish. Tony would get an order from a restaurant. He would write down the order on a Formica plate so we could take it down with us as a menu—like how many groupers, amberjacks, and bream."

Ray explained how they would always go out to the Bank, to the Munxar, which always had fish. And since fish brought big money, the divers took extraordinary measures to protect their areas—sometimes even taking extra tanks so they could dive down in one area for the benefit of the people watching on shore and then swim underwater to the real fishing spots. This sleight of hand would entertain the tourists—who thought that's where the good fish were—and would throw those with prying eyes off the divers' trail. Theirs was a secretive group, and by the tone of Ray's voice they remained so even today.

"The anchors you speak of, Bob—" Ray continued—"this could be trouble, big trouble, for anyone who possesses an ancient artifact. There are strict laws about that in Malta. There could be a big fine. It could mean...*jail*."

In spite of Ray's assurance that none among his old diving fraternity would likely volunteer information about the anchors, I asked anyway. "Could you put me in touch with Joe Navarro," I asked, recalling the diver who helped Tony bring up the intact second anchor from the Munxar Reef.

Ray paused and stared off in the distance. Finally he exhaled, nodded, and said, "I will see what I can do."

JOE NAVARRO

I met with Joe Navarro in the courtyard of my hotel, beneath a hot sun and draping palm trees. I opened with a few questions about the diving culture on the Malta of his youth and he reflexively replied, "There were a lot of accidents in those days—a lack of safety."

Once a diving instructor in Tony's dive club, Joe ultimately grew out of his obsession and studied to become a schoolteacher. "I try to impart logic and reason to my students," he said. "As they go through life, they will encounter many circumstances and situations that could cause them harm." He locked me with a stare and then added, "I have brought several people out of the water who died from being foolish."

One of these "foolish" incidents, he recalled, involved an ill-trained Englishman who went diving in the local waters, regurgitated into his regulator, and choked to death. Joe shook his head. "He was in only *ten feet* of water."

Another accident took a top Maltese underwater fishing champion. "He must have blacked out," Joe recalled. "But, then again, those were dangerous days. I have personally brought three people up from the bottom. I always wanted to put the fear of the Lord into these guys who were underwater cowboys, *you know?*"

Inevitably the talk turned to Tony. Joe laughed, recalling a rather bizarre incident in which Tony, fishing one afternoon near the reef, heard a succession of underwater explosions. I watched Joe's eyes grow wide as he explained. "When Tony came to the surface, he saw some guy exploding *dynamite* in the water to catch fish. Tony shouted to the man, "You almost *killed* me with your dynamite!" The man said simply, 'You're fishing. I'm fishing.'"

Finally, I asked Joe about Tony and the anchors Ray had mentioned.

"I know of an anchor that came out of the Munxar Reef," he said, "because I was part of the group of people who brought it out."

He related the episode as he remembered it, describing in detail how Tony told him that he had discovered a Roman anchor in front of the big cave on the Munxar Reef and that they all conspired to bring it up with oxygen tanks and empty barrels. As Joe told me about the barrels filling with air and slowly lifting the anchor, he recalled the tension.

"It felt like the anchor was protesting our intrusion. I thought the ropes were going to snap, but then it budged from its sandy hold, and I saw this huge anchor that had belonged to the sea for so long inching its way up. At first it nudged just a few centimeters, then it came loose in a swirl of sand—like after two thousand years the ocean suddenly lost its grip on a prize. Once it cleared the bottom, we knew it no longer belonged to the sea—it belonged to us."

Even decades later, Joe described it as, "the most exciting moment of my life—watching as the anchor rose to the surface, the bubbles from the divers and the trailing sand swirling behind it. From the bottom I watched as the anchor was carried up into the sunlight."

But even with Joe's exhilaration, I could sense unease. I could tell that the joy of the moment had been tarnished somewhat by the sense that they had done something wrong. "As I watched this thing, so old, so magnificent, taken from the seabed," Joe said, shifting in his chair, "I felt as if I was treading on something...*sacred.*"

When I explained my theory about the anchor possibly being one of four from Paul's shipwreck, Joe sat without speaking for some time.

"What do you think about that?" I finally asked, expecting that he might pass judgment on the theory itself. But he surprised me instead with what sounded like...a belated apology.

He mumbled softly, "What we did was wrong, whether the anchor was from St. Paul's shipwreck or not. It belonged to the ocean...pulling the anchor up like that was like grave-robbing, like a sacrilege. I wish now that we had left the anchor at rest on the seafloor."

And then he said something I didn't expect. "I have *seen* the anchor since that day...at Tony's house. But it really belongs to the ocean."

Tony's house? The *anchor* at Tony's house? I let the comment pass— temporarily. I would have to inquire about this remark later. Joe struck me as both honest and sincere, someone who had some youthful regrets from a heady and dangerous season of life. I thanked him for the interview. He nodded and said, "I have a brother, you know. He was there when they melted the first cut anchor. I am sure he would be willing to tell you about his experience."

MESSAGE FROM A MELTED ANCHOR

Later that night, I met Oliver Navarro for dinner in a restaurant called The Black Pearl, a massive, converted wooden ship that had been built in Sweden in 1909. I'm told it was once owned by Errol Flynn and had been used as a prop in the movie *Popeye,* starring Robin Williams. It sat still adorned with rustic beams and weathered planking; I felt like we were dining in the bowels of an old pirate ship.

We had barely finished the introductions when Oliver reached into a small bag and lifted out a square block of lead, placing it in the middle of the candlelit table. "I was a young man about the same age as Ray when I met Tony," he said. "The best times of my life were spent with Tony—he was an excellent man. We started doing competitions together; you know, dive competitions, spearfishing and the like." He chuckled. "I couldn't keep up with him."

Oliver told me about the day in the dive shop when Tony spoke of finding something "really nice, really beautiful" near the underwater cave and then proceeded to show Oliver what looked like a big piece of stone with a square hole in the middle.

"I was maybe fourteen, fifteen years old, and didn't know much about archaeology," Oliver said. "They all told me it was a Roman anchor that had a piece cut from it. I figured that before it was cut it must have been maybe five feet long. They said the square hole in the middle was where the wooden shaft would have fit in."

And then—just as Ray and others had explained—Oliver said that lead was in high demand in those days; they used it to make small weights for diving belts. "The weights were always getting misplaced or lost beneath the waves," he said, "always slipping from the deck of a boat, always difficult to replace."

He told me that Tony and the others decided to melt down this big lead anchor to make weights, figuring that since someone had already cut it in half, it had lost whatever value it once held. "And besides," he added, "If the museum found out we had it, we would be in a bit of trouble. So one afternoon we just started cutting on this big lead thing. Ray and I cut it with hacksaw blades until our hands almost bled."

His voice grew soft, like his brother Joe's. "We all needed the lead for weights; but silently I think we all felt like we were killing this thing, this thing that was two thousand years old."

The process he described sounded, indeed, like a primitive slaughter of sorts, with gas bottles hissing and hacksaws carving off chips and pieces that were unceremoniously tossed into black, smoldering pots for meltdown. "Smoke was swirling from the garage," he said, "and we had to stand back because of the vapors. When chunks fell into the melted lead, some would splatter out. We had to use tongs to hold the molds as the lead was poured from the pots."

Oliver reached down and grabbed the weight from the table in front of me; he held it up to the candlelight.

"This is one of two weights that were given to me by Tony that day," he said. "I'm sure others exist around Malta. Or maybe they too have been lost in the sea by careless divers. But this is one of my two that survives."

He set the weight down, and I reached over and grabbed it. The dense cool mass felt much heavier than I anticipated. I remembered Ray telling me that he had chiseled TM into the molds that day—TM, for Tony Micallef-Borg. I wanted to find one of those old weights! This one appeared to be bare; it had no markings. But as I pulled it close to the candle, I saw the letters *MT*. I placed the weight back onto the table and said to Oliver, "Ray told me that on the day the anchor was melted, he took a hammer and chiseled *TM* into the mold." I showed him the initials. "This one says MT."

"He did," Oliver laughed. "We all watched him do it. It surprised us when the weights came out MT. When we poured the lead into the mold and pulled out the weights, the TM became the reverse—*MT*."

TORN IN TWO

I knew that I had to begin interviewing the other eyewitnesses Ray and others said were involved in the recovery and melting of the so-called cut anchor. The whole affair raised a nagging question: When they found the anchor, it appeared to have been cut—on the seafloor—but who would cut an anchor at the bottom of the sea?

Hoping to find a logical answer, I tracked down Charlie Vella, an eyewitness who helped Tony bring up the first anchor. We met at a seaside restaurant in beautiful St. Julian's Bay. He was tanned, with a short, gray beard, and looked to be in exceptional shape. As we talked and slowly became acquainted, he too began reminiscing about the fellowship of early divers on Malta. Charlie told me that Tony had been his PE teacher in school.

"I'd been getting in a little trouble," he said quietly. "Tony took it upon himself to mentor me, just like he mentored Ray and many other students."

I wasn't the least bit surprised to find that Charlie held as much affection for Tony as everyone else on the island seemed to. Like the others, Charlie had his own spin on the Tony legend.

"He was a special guy," Charlie said, "always taking students camping, helping them out, keeping them out of trouble. That's how he got me interested in diving at the Cresta Quay Dive School. I later became an instructor, and then a professional diver."

Charlie told me that he had become one of the first international "saturation divers"—a commercial diver who takes on special, high-risk jobs in extremely deep waters. The job had left him with some incredible memories, and for the next hour he cheerfully regaled me with tales of his "deep dives," including one particularly harrowing experience in 1979, working northwest of Spain at Christmastime. He had taken on a job to change a hydraulic hose that had burst at the base of an oilrig in eight hundred feet of water. He didn't know that he had placed his life in the hands of an inexperienced crew until it was almost too late.

"I was eight hundred feet down, in pitch-black darkness, walking on the bottom of the ocean with only a headlamp illuminating the way," he began. "The temperature was between four and five degrees centigrade, a numbing, unbearable cold. The hot water heating system, which pumped hot water through my special diving suit, suddenly stopped working. It just *quit!*"

Charlie was forced to drag himself along the seafloor, the heavy lead weights on his legs feeling like anvils, to climb back up into the diving bell that had transported him to the bottom. There, he expected to find the artificial warmth that would save his life—but the hot water system in the dive chamber had stopped working as well. He ordered the crew to bring him up—a process that takes considerable time under the best of conditions, much less with systems failing. With a grim countenance Charlie said, "I almost died from hypothermia by the time I reached the surface."

To compound matters, the crew had mismanaged the mixture of oxygen and helium used in his decompression, keeping him trapped inside the diving bell for several hours after he reached the deck of the ship. Charlie clearly took some pride in the fact that he never lost consciousness or awareness of his predicament during the ordeal, though he demonstrated how he was still shaking uncontrollably by the time he left the bell. That had been a close call; he had come perilously close to joining his many friends who had succumbed to the perils of deep-water diving.

A highly trained and experienced diver, Charlie was a man who kept his wits about him and, even on dry land, remained acutely aware of his surroundings. When he described something on the ocean floor, I had no doubt about its accuracy. When it came to diving, here was a fellow who knew what he was talking about. As our conversation returned to the discovery of the first anchor, I asked Charlie why he thought some of the divers believed the anchor had been cut. Was it sawn in two? Had it been moved? What did he think had happened to it?

"It was obvious what had happened," Charlie said. "The anchor had literally been *ripped* in half." Pointing to my notebook, he said, "Let me show you."

Sliding my notebook across the table, I watched him take a pen from his shirt pocket and begin sketching a rough image of that first anchor, long since melted into diving weights. With nothing to go on but one palm-sized weight, I knew that Charlie's picture would come closer than anything else to seeing the actual artifact that had gripped the imagination of that fraternity of early divers.

Charlie sketched quickly, turning the page as he went, and then suddenly pronounced his artwork finished. "There!" he said, sliding the notebook back to me.

What I saw on that small notebook page explained everything. The picture was of a Roman anchor stock identical to the others we had discovered in our search, only half gone. From Charlie's drawing, however, it appeared as if the anchor had not been *cut* so much as stressed, stretched, distorted. It looked like it had, after some great, forceful violence, simply broken at its weakest point. His drawing looked as if the anchor had been pulled apart like a piece of taffy, precisely at the place where the stock was thinnest—where the wooden main shaft of the anchor would pass through.[18]

Stunned by the drawing, I didn't know what to make of Charlie's implication. The amount of force necessary to twist and break a thick, heavy lead anchor off its stock would be enormous. I couldn't begin to picture it in my mind, though Charlie seemed quite confident that it was exactly what had happened.

I cleared my throat. "What do you think could have done *that?* What could produce that kind of force?"

Charlie didn't hesitate, having clearly thought it through many times. "It could only have been a violent, terrible storm that was ripping at a ship out there on the Munxar," he said, raising his eyebrows at the prospect. "What an incredible force it must have been that could do something like that!"

I let Charlie's words simmer in my mind. Was it possible? Could a mere *storm* have produced enough force to snap off an anchor? A few more moments passed. I stared at the distorted, sheared anchor stock Charlie had sketched from memory. It was then that I realized that there was probably only one possible explanation for its presence on the outer Munxar, as well as its condition.

"This was probably the first anchor thrown out as a ship tried to stop its momentum and stay off the rocks," I whispered, almost to myself.

I'd witnessed the fury of the Malta Sea—the raw, grinding force of the waves, which could beach a modern cargo ship and then pound it to pieces. Finally, I began to understand that every treatment of Acts 27 probably *undersold* what actually happened that night on the outer Munxar. A gregale is the most feared, powerful, and deadly storm known in the Mediterranean. Sitting there imagining it, as Charlie continued talking about some other diving exploits of his and Tony's, I kept drifting back to the horrific storm described in Acts.

Paul and his companions had been locked in its grip for two weeks, and the ship was still being tossed like a toy in heavy seas. As the starving, weary, hopeless human cargo held on for dear life in the darkness, they began to hear the sound of water exploding somewhere off in the blackness around them.

Fighting fear and the elements, they threw one or more of the lead-weighted lines that had been knotted at standard intervals, gauging the depth first at twenty fathoms, then at fifteen fathoms. Their ears weren't deceiving them—they were headed straight for land. By now the roaring explosion of the shallow Munxar was beside them as well as in front of them, and the swells grew even taller as they stacked up on the shallow bottom. To drop anchors from the bow and let the ship weathervane all the way around would be suicide. So groups of soldiers, crewmen, and prisoners probably began working frantically on the pitching deck, moving anchors from their stowage on the bow to the far stern of the ship. They had only one chance to stop the ship in its tracks and hoped that the anchors would hold.

We can only imagine the wrenching, crashing, terrifying impact on that single anchor, tied off on the gunwales and thrown into the raging sea, as it suddenly "bit" on the bottom and pulled the massive rope taut. The violent pull must have strained every board and beam on the storm-beaten ship and sent men and equipment flying forward. Then, just as suddenly as it pulled tight, the anchor (according to Charlie's drawing) would have literally broken loose, ravaged by the reef and the waves. This probably sent a wave of panic through the men as they struggled to heave a second, then a third, and finally a fourth anchor overboard. Only as the other anchors bit and held did the first anchor settle to the bottom as well. Now, however, only three-and-a-half anchors held the ship off the rocks until daylight revealed the gloomy scene Luke described in Acts.

Could it really have happened that way? Perhaps, perhaps not. But lined up next to the countless theories surmising on the location and nature of Paul's shipwreck on Malta, this was, finally, one scenario that fit the vast preponderance of evidence. All the physical landmarks precisely matched Luke's description—from the anchors found on the outer Munxar, to the broken anchor found among them, to the depth of the sea and the presence of the reef itself.

For an object that no longer existed in its original form, these spontaneous musings about the "melted anchor" had done more to validate our search than anything I had been able to actually see and touch. From Charlie's vivid description of the anchor, it was evident that some ship—though not necessarily *Paul's* ship—had been in a violent storm and had dropped an anchor in front of the Munxar Reef. The force of that storm, as amazing as it sounded, may well have torn the lead stock of that anchor in two, which raised an interesting question: *In the absence of a violent storm, why would the captain of any ship have intentionally dropped an anchor in front of a reef seething with violent waves? All other things being equal, wouldn't he seek a place offering more protection, a familiar harbor away from the violence of waves crashing upon a reef?*

The fact is, a seasoned captain would never have chosen that bay, or that reef, to drop anchor—unless he had no choice. It now seemed obvious that the anchor had been dropped from a ship that had come upon this reef without design or purpose. The captain faced a hopeless situation. He had anchored his ship in such a deadly location, in the teeth of a formidable reef, only *because he had to.*

Weighing these factors, I concluded that if all of the anchors found near the big cave had come from the same ship, it only made sense they had been dropped during a storm. They must have been cast out in desperation, from a ship fighting for its very survival in a merciless storm.

A FAMILY HEIRLOOM

The following day Ray called me at my hotel with a surprise. He said I could see the anchor that he, Tony, and Joe had brought up from the Munxar. With no more information than that, I herded my research team in the van and drove quickly to the dive shop, where Ray was waiting with his fiancée, Jo.

"It will be a lot quicker if I drive." Ray smiled as he and Jo slid into the front seat of the van. The Maltese landscape flew past the windows as Ray sped down unmarked country roads and through several rural villages, slowing only as we approached a small cluster of sun-washed villas.

"The team will have to wait here," Ray said as he pulled over to the side of the road, about a hundred yards from the picturesque row of little villas. "We don't want to make Margaret nervous." In his every movement, I could sense Ray's reverence for Tony's widow as he, Jo, and I walked up to the heavy wooden front door.

Ray knocked on the door, and after a few seconds a dignified-looking woman appeared and greeted us warmly, then invited us inside. As we entered the front parlor, Margaret hugged Ray and Jo and gave them a kiss on each cheek, the typical Maltese greeting. Margaret poured us tea and served cake, moving with grace and elegance around the tastefully decorated villa. I took instant notice of her kind eyes—they revealed a gentle spirit, but could not completely veil the pain of the past.

After several minutes of small talk, she looked over at me and asked, "Would you like to see Tony's anchor?"

Ray had obviously smoothed my way with Margaret, but I didn't want to take advantage of her eager trust. Tony's death had affected the whole island, but no one had suffered as much as this gentle woman, who never expected to have an outsider like me asking her about the old anchor.

"Before I do," I said with a smile, "I'd like you to know why we are so interested in the anchor your husband found." I explained the research we had done and shared our fast-evolving theory about the object Tony had brought up—that it was quite possibly one of the four anchors from Paul's shipwreck.

She didn't show a hint of surprise, answering simply, "That would be just like Tony. If anyone would come across Paul's shipwreck, it would be my Tony." She grinned and added, "He was quite special, you know."

"That's what I have heard," I replied. "I've been told that your husband was a remarkable man.

"Yes, I think he would be proud to know that he had been a part of such a discovery."

Margaret reached out and touched me gently on the arm. "Tony found the anchor and brought it up," she said, "so it means a lot to me. I can see now that maybe it will be important to others. But for me it will always be a memento of him, something that he brought home from the

125

sea. But—" she paused, searching for words—"I am afraid... *concerned*... that if the authorities find out about it, they will come and take it away. That would mean serious trouble for me. I will show you the anchor, but I worry about what may happen."

I followed Margaret down a hallway leading into a sun-drenched courtyard, which was open to the sky and framed by carefully tended flower-filled gardens. She gently motioned to the front part of the court-yard: There, lying on the polished floor, laid the anchor. It was a large slab of lead, encrusted with dried sea growth. Narrow slits in its side revealed the scars of two millennia of exposure to the constant currents of the sea.

I bent down and ran my hand over the cool leaden mass, my thoughts alive with images of sailors standing in wind and rain on the deck of a tempest-tossed ship. A desperate crew had perhaps strained to throw this very anchor over the side in a final attempt to hold the ship fast before it ran aground.

Could this really be an anchor from Paul's ship? I asked myself. Everything seemed to add up: It was the right object, from the right place, and apparently from the right era of history and even from the right depth of the ocean. I took my time examining the anchor, reminding myself that the ancient object in front of me represented only the second anchor pulled from the waters of Munxar Reef. I lowered my hand to touch the cool lead and felt as if my hand lay upon an object that spanned the ages. *Was I actually touching a physical connection to Paul himself?* I couldn't let the emotion of the moment cloud the reality of the task before me.

I had patiently followed a path that led me to this massive Roman anchor stock, and the journey had taught me just how difficult it could be to follow a cold trail through the close-knit communities of Malta.

These people, like indigenous cultures around the world, watch out for each other, protect each other, and can be as secretive as they need to be in order to take care of their own.

Only simple trust, the hope of friendship, and brutal honesty had brought me this far. Ray had opened up to me some of the most intimate, painful memories of his life; now Margaret offered us not only the hospitality of her home but also held out to a complete stranger one of the prized mementos belonging to her late husband.

Kneeling beside that ancient slab of lead, I sensed that the same simple inquiry and analysis that had brought us this far would keep the plot moving forward. I explained to Margaret that I had invited a scholar along who could greatly assist my research.

She thought for a moment and said, "If it is important, he may see the anchor."

Dr. Mark Phillips soon joined us in the courtyard. Margaret had given me permission to photograph and videotape the anchor, and as I panned the camera over it from different angles, Mark literally gawked in amazement at what he was seeing. He wasted no time postulating that it could very well be a Roman anchor, possibly even forged during Paul's era, but dating the anchor precisely lay beyond his expertise.

Mark then turned to me saying, "My wife and I are having dinner with Professor Anthony Bonanno and his wife, and you must join us." I knew Professor Bonanno to be a local professor and head of the Department of Archaeology at the University of Malta. Mark suggested we show the professor the video of the anchor and ask his opinion.

I thanked Margaret again for her kindness in allowing us this rare opportunity. The promise I had made to keep this secret would be fulfilled. But in my wildest imagination I couldn't have predicted where the adventure would lead from here.

THE PROFESSOR

Professor Anthony Bonanno is considered to be the foremost expert in Malta on Roman antiquities. Having earned a Ph.D. from the prestigious University of London Institute of Archeology, Professor Bonanno has taught at the University of Malta since 1971. He regularly lectures at European universities on Maltese archaeological heritage and has convened two important international conferences on Maltese archaeology.[19] I looked forward to presenting my theory and hearing his response, knowing there would be unavoidable consequences either way.

My scheduled stay in Malta was drawing to a close. Our investigation had moved in an entirely unforeseen direction—from sea to land. Our dive team had fulfilled its purpose, and I knew it was time to return to Colorado and regroup. I joined Dr. Phillips and his wife, Angela, along with Professor Bonanno at the hotel restaurant just as they were ordering their meal.

Mark wasted no time. Before *we* had even ordered, he asked me to show Professor Bonanno the video of Margaret's anchor. I pulled out a tiny video from my briefcase, flipped up the screen, and pressed play. The LCD screen flickered to life with images of the anchor. Professor Bonanno knew immediately what the object was.

"What you have just shown me," he said, "appears to be an anchor. To be more precise, it is part of the anchor known as an anchor stock, commonly used on Roman vessels. Of course, I cannot say for a certain from a video. I would have to physically examine the artifact and conduct further tests.

"Could this be from an Alexandrian grain freighter?" I asked.

"It could have been from a Roman/Alexandrian grain freighter," he replied.

"What would you say is the probable dating of the anchor?"

"Anchor stocks such as the one you are showing me in this video were used from approximately 100 B.C. to 100 A.D.," said Professor Bonanno. "It could have come from any period within that range."

When asked if it were possible for that anchor to have come from the era of the shipwreck of St. Paul, in 60 A.D., Professor Bonanno replied that from what he could tell from the video, it was consistent with an anchor of that era, however without an identifying mark of some type, it would be impossible to be more specific.

Professor Bonanno's observations were astounding! I couldn't help noticing the smile on Dr. Phillips's face.

I wish I could have enjoyed more of the evening's conversation, but I regrettably had to excuse myself from the group in order to catch my evening flight for London. In London, I would take the early morning flight to the United States on United Airlines flight 929—September 11, 2001.

As I made my way to the airport, through passport control, and onto the airplane, I couldn't help but replay in my mind the varied and unpredictable route our expedition had taken. Before the plane lifted off the runway, I had already begun to plan my next trip to Malta.

I knew that the next phase would require good solid detective work, which added considerably to my excitement. I had come to Malta this time with a dive team, expecting to work out of my element, exploring the floor of the Mediterranean Sea. Now I had a whole new strategy to pursue as an investigator, a style far more familiar to me. I would come back to Malta and follow-up on Ray's tip about the two more anchors taken from the Munxar.

Could I find any remaining evidence of the melted anchor? Could I track down any eyewitness testimony concerning additional anchors? Would I be able to follow the trail of the two remaining anchors—if they existed—and earn the trust of their owners? And, most importantly, would I be able to find the common thread connecting all four anchors not only to each other, but also to that one spot on the Munxar, where I had grown more convinced that Paul's ship ran aground? ⚓

Chapter Eleven

AN UNEXPECTED LANDING

OVER THE ATLANTIC—SEPTEMBER 11, 2001

*f*lying at thirty-nine thousand feet above the Atlantic, the Boeing 777 cabin was stone silent except for the droning of engines cutting through the frigid upper atmosphere. All the passengers were unaware the crew had just been notified only minutes prior that passenger airplanes in U.S. airspace were being hijacked and flown into buildings. All our lives were forever altered in that moment of impact—when the first plane rammed into the World Trade Center. Little could I imagine how it would change my life and the search for the anchors. A miniature video screen on the back of the seat in front of me told me we had four and half hours left on this mundane flight from London to Chicago. I could see from the map on the screen that we were approaching Newfoundland on the northeast coast of Canada.

A friend of mine once referred to a jet passenger plane as a huge, hermetically sealed tube. The exits are virtually useless unless you are safely stopped on the ground or above the waterline. When you enter a plane and seatbelt yourself in, you are in the position of totally trusting people you have never met, and probably will never meet, trusting that someone has filled it with jet fuel, installed the engines correctly, and properly maintained them. You are hoping, of course, that the pilot is not only highly trained and experienced, but has also had a zillion hours of combat flight and knows what to do in any possible emergency situation. Belted in at thirty-nine thousand feet, a person has no choice but to trust completely.

Suddenly, there came such a violent buffeting through the cabin that the overhead bins popped open. Flight attendants grabbed on to the bulkheads, and the plane started to drop like a rock. There was a thunderous noise of wind and mechanical vibration, and the plane started shaking. The video screen on the back of the seat in front of me displayed thirty-nine thousand feet…thirty-seven thousand…thirty-five thousand…thirty-two thousand…. The loudspeaker crackled on with the pilot's voice telling us that there was some kind of "situation" and that he would get back to us with an update. His stream of words seemed compressed and hurried, giving the distinct impression that United Flight 929 was in serious trouble. The flight attendants pulled themselves up the aisles against the violently shaking craft and the gravity of the descent, shouting, "Put your seats up! Put your seatbelts on! Put your shoes on!" The man seated next to me leaned over and said calmly, "We have about four to five minutes before we hit the Atlantic Ocean."

At just that moment, however, the captain came back on the intercom to say, in a steadied voice, "Nothing is wrong with the aircraft, but we will have to make an immediate landing on the island of Newfoundland." The map on the screen in front of me showed that Newfoundland is located just southeast of Greenland. No one spoke. I could see the white knuckles of those around me hanging on to armrests, anxiety etched into their furrowed brows. Then came the chilling words from the intercom above us: "Uh, folks, there has been an incident…a major emergency in the United States. All of the U.S. and Canadian borders are closed to approaching aircraft…and we have been ordered to land in Gander immediately."

Then people started to talk. A buzz filled the airplane from one end to the other. What had happened? What could be so major that it would close the U.S. and Canadian borders? I heard whispers throughout the cabin, suggesting anything from nuclear attack to an outbreak of war. In a matter of moments, we had become literally suspended between two worlds: the safe world we left a few hours before in London and some kind of weird, surreal, unknown world that we were traveling into. One of the passengers later told me that jet fuel had been dumped, streaming from the wings in a liquid mass swirling into a trailing spray.

As we descended the pilot lowered the landing gear, creating a condition called "dirty air"—a maneuver pilots use to drop the aircraft's altitude rapidly. I learned later that one of the reasons we descended to the ground so quickly was because our flight crew had no way of knowing whether or not we had terrorists onboard who were planning to take over the plane.

The landing was a blur. I saw the Newfoundland coastline, and then in the next moment, it seemed, felt the wheels hit the runway with a thud as the engines reversed and the plane dipped down against the pressure of the brakes. As the plane slowed, everyone aboard breathed a sigh of relief, though our minds were still racing with the possible scenario that had brought us from thirty-nine thousand feet to the runway in only a matter of minutes.

GANDER, NEWFOUNDLAND—SEPTEMBER 11, 2001

Immediately passengers began using cell phones to contact loved ones, to find out what had happened in the United States to create such an emergency. One by one people would shout out updates: "One plane struck the World Trade Center...two planes..." Then we heard "Pittsburgh..." Then the "Pentagon..." Then we heard the word *terrorists*. The man behind me turned to his wife and said, "I hope he's okay." I later learned that his son-in-law was in the World Trade Center. The captain told us that we could listen to the BBC on channel eight of the console radio. Everybody slid on their headphones and listened to the reports from London of the incredible tragedy unfolding back at home.

In my hurry to get to the airport in Malta the night before, I did not call my wife and tell her of my travel plans. I had planned to surprise her at her class reunion in Milwaukee. She would have no way of knowing that I now sat on a runway in Newfoundland, or that I was even flying home at that time. A lady offered me the use of her cell phone, so I called Terry, who was staying with our children at her parents' house in Milwaukee. Thinking I was in Malta, she asked, "Have you heard the news?"

"Yes," I said. "I'm in Gander, Newfoundland."

"Gander?" She was startled. "What are you doing there?"

"They diverted us here because..." I attempted to explain.

"I know," she interrupted. "I know."

Not wanting to drain the time or battery from the borrowed cell phone, I told Terry that I would need to call her back when I could and that I would be okay.

"I understand," she said.

As I looked out my window at the scene around us, I could see many other commercial and military planes spread around the airport, with more landing every few minutes—but, strangely, with none of the ground support equipment normally accompanying that kind of traffic. Lined up along the runways and the taxiways, the growing collection of planes displayed a huge variety of airline insignias and countries of origin. In all, some thirty-eight large civilian planes would eventually be lined up along the tarmac, wingtip to wingtip. The entire population of Gander is only ten thousand, but now more than seven thousand people—stranded passengers from around the world—sat in airliners on the runway. Through my window I watched as a steady stream of curious onlookers gathered behind a chain-link fence alongside the airport to witness this one-time, historical event. Just hours before, Gander was nothing more than a nondescript, anonymous little town; now it seemed as if half the world had descended upon it from out of the blue.

The pilot told us he would give us periodic updates, but for now we would have to "sit tight." So that's what we did. We just sat, and sat. We had landed sometime around noon, and it was a hot day for that late in the season. Adding to our discomfort, the plane's air conditioning gave out. Only when the sun, arcing low across the sky, finally set did we find a bit of relief from our confinement.

As the hours crept by, the plane's supplies were being exhausted until there was no food or drinks except for the liquor cabinet, which was locked for obvious reasons. Even the cups ran out, so each of us wrote our name on a single Styrofoam cup, which we kept in order to get an occasional drink of water. In all, we sat on the plane for a total of twenty-six hours from the time of takeoff to the time we finally deplaned in Newfoundland. I found it reassuring, given the horror going on in the United States, that not one person complained or caused any kind of problem.

Boarding United Flight 929 in London, we all took it for granted that we would be disembarking in Chicago. Instead, the terrorist attacks made us temporary refugees, waiting to be processed into Newfoundland through Canadian customs. The reentry took us through rigorous check-points, where customs officials and Royal Canadian Mounted Police officers tore through our bags one by one. In the days and weeks after 9/11, so many people were being processed that exhausted officials worked double and triple shifts.

Once we cleared customs, we were each handed a small sub sandwich, a bottle of water, and a piece of cold pizza. Then they herded us to school buses for transfer to makeshift accommodations. The buses transported our planeload of 198 passengers thirty minutes south of Gander to the small fishing village of Gambo.

GAMBO, NEWFOUNDLAND—SEPTEMBER 12, 2001

In Gambo, we arrived at a Salvation Army church, where workers handed everyone a blanket and told us to find a place to sleep on one of the pews or on the floor. By the time everyone bedded down that night, the church had been filled wall-to-wall with marooned travelers. Looking out the church window and down the road, I saw a small white house with a satellite dish bolted on the side.

Why not? I said to myself.

I left the church and walked down the road and up the steps to the little house and knocked gently on the front door. A woman answered, looked me up and down, and said, "You're one of the people from the airplanes, aren't you?"

"Yes, I am," I said, looking as dejected as I could.

"Well, you just come in and make yourself at home," she said. "We were hoping we could help in some way."

Harold and Madelaine immediately adopted me. Harold was an eighty-two-year-old retired cod fisherman; Madelaine was twenty-five years his junior, and they boasted of having twelve children, all of whom had moved away. She led me into the living room and said, "Can I feed you anything?"

Again, trying to look dejected, I said, "Please don't bother."

Well, that was all it took. In an instant, cod sizzled in a skillet, cookies rose in the oven, and CNN, with all its unfolding coverage, flickered on the television. I made a collect call to my wife and updated her about my new residence in Gambo. She immediately asked to talk to Madelaine and told her not to fuss or go to any trouble.

"Don't you worry about a thing," Madelaine said. "He's being well taken care of. He's working on his second plateful of cod right now."

Madelaine handed the phone back to me, and Terry said, with all sympathy now gone from her voice, "It sounds like you're taken care of."

I would spend the next five days in Gambo, amazed by the people of the town and their hospitality. Hundreds of people brought food, clothing, and medicine to the stranded passengers. We were not allowed to take any of our luggage off the airplane, so we were stranded without anything. Yet the townsfolk of Gambo supplied everything we really needed. I remember thinking at the time that even though September 11 unveiled the brutality of fanatics with a misguided cause, it also showed the goodness that can emerge in the face of a crisis.

Five days later we finally returned to Chicago, where we learned that we were the last stranded United Airlines flight to return to the United States. Our flight crew—which for nearly a week had gone far beyond anything normally expected of an airline's employees—taxied our plane through a corridor of ground crew and other personnel waving American flags, finally delivering us to our gate and our waiting loved ones.

Aside from the hospitality we encountered, the layover in Newfoundland allowed me to really ponder the implications of the shipwreck of Paul. *If we were really on to the correct location, and if the anchor I saw just a few days earlier was one of the shipwreck's actual anchors, then what would this all mean to me, to the world, to those studying and contemplating the historical truths of the Bible?*

In a strange sort of way, I began identifying with many things those aboard Paul's ship must have experienced. I was traveling from Malta to Chicago and wound up on an island called Newfoundland. Paul's ship was traveling from Caesarea to Rome and wound up on the island of Malta. Paul's ship carried 276 people; our airplane carried a total of 215 people. Sensing imminent peril as we approached the island, I checked the altitude of the plane; sensing the peril of running aground as they approached their island, the sailors on Paul's ship took depth soundings. We had dumped fuel into the ocean to make our craft lighter for landing; on Paul's ship they dumped grain into the sea to make the ship lighter for their intended landing. After landfall the natives on Malta treated Paul's group with amazing kindness; after our landing we were treated with similar kindness as refugees in Newfoundland. The similarities seemed fairly amusing to me.

I was looking forward to returning to the familiar confines of my office in Colorado Springs, where I could reflect, regroup, and rethink everything that had happened since I first left from Malta some six days earlier.

Chapter Twelve

AFGHAN ODYSSEY

*T*he chaos surrounding the September 11 terrorist attacks temporarily sidetracked my search for Paul's sea anchors. By the end of my surprisingly pleasant Newfoundland layover, having finally made my way back to the U.S., a new vernacular had crept into the national vocabulary. Words like *Taliban, Al-Qaida, Ground Zero,* and *War on Terror* now assumed a prominent place in our everyday lives. In the weeks following September 11, our culture found itself on unfamiliar psychological terrain, with millions of ordinary citizens suddenly paralyzed at the prospect of opening an envelope, turning on a water tap, or boarding an airplane. Beyond our collective rage at Osama Bin Ladin, America's focus turned to the sinister threat of a group of previously ignored fanatics living secretly among us. Images of fire, destruction, and death played out thousands of times on our television screens, and the certainty of war became a morbid fact of life.

Fear eventually gave way to cries for vengeance. Evil had had its day, but not its way. A powerful new brand of patriotism sprang to life, and our public sadness and mourning drifted irreversibly toward national resolve.

I had been home less than two months when I received a phone call from a man named Jerry Rose. President of the Total Living Network in Chicago, Jerry asked me if I might be willing to travel to Afghanistan, of all places, to take part in a special film project. Jerry knew that I had spent much of the past seventeen years crisscrossing the Middle East; apparently he felt that I had the skills and abilities to get us into Afghanistan and navigate through a treacherous, wartime situation. With a bloody war against the Taliban now raging full-tilt in that besieged country, "treacherous" seemed a monumental understatement.

By then life had returned to a semblance of normalcy. I had turned my full-time attention back to the Malta project, running my ministry—BASE Institute—and juggling several other time-consuming projects. Even though it would be for a worthwhile project, I didn't think I could pull away for the length of time Jerry described. The brutality of the Taliban had become a tormenting cancer to a people already weary from hundreds of years of wars, and Jerry wanted me to help videotape relief efforts taking place amid the falling bombs. He reasoned that millions of people would be inspired by video of aid being clandestinely taken to people victimized by their own leaders, and I had to agree—it had the makings of a poignant story of good versus evil, the kind of a tale I loved being part of.

It would be a hard decision since I would need to leave within the next two weeks. I told Jerry I would have to get back to him.

PRISONERS OF HOPE

Two days later, I received a phone call from Dayna Curry and Heather Mercer. Just weeks earlier, I had seen the two women interviewed on CNN after they were rescued by Special Forces in a daring escape from their imprisonment by the Taliban. For weeks the world held its breath as these young missionaries, along with a few others, were held by their Taliban captors and used as pawns in a savage war. I remember seeing the news reports during their captivity and thinking, *These young women probably won't survive.*

During our phone conversation, Heather and Dayna told me how they had risked their lives helping Afghan women who were being tortured, tormented, and persecuted by the Taliban. They shared some of the details of their amazing escape. Here again, their story struck a familiar chord: Much like how Paul had been miraculously saved on Malta, God held the impossible in His hand. Heather and Dayna said a mutual friend had informed them that I might be going to Afghanistan. They wanted to know if I could possibly help them tell their story. It seems that in fleeing for their lives, they had left their journals in Kabul.

"Will you be going to Kabul?" Dayna inquired. "Could you try to find the journals we left behind and photograph the prison and the home where we lived in Kabul?"

I told them that if I decided to go to Afghanistan, I would do my best to help them. That night I weighed the decision whether or not to go. After much prayer, the answer came from my wife, Terry, who always shares from her heart on these matters. "You'll never have this opportunity again, Bob," she said. "This is the event of our lifetime. Our parents had World War II; we have September 11."

Terry never fails to surprise me. She has encouraged me to find unique ways to inspire others, even though it may involve travel to some dangerous, American-hating countries. I have often joked that she has our life insurance agent on speed dial, but the simple truth is that she recognizes that I was created for this kind of work. When I asked her why Afghanistan, especially now, she replied calmly, "Because I believe in you. I believe that you can do what they want you to do. And I know that this story will be an encouragement to so many." My wife is an amazing woman.

Just days later, I kissed and hugged my family good-bye at Denver International Airport. Though I could see in their eyes a deep concern, even my children wore brave smiles. As I walked toward my flight, I tried to think, *It will only be two weeks before I come home again.*

I met up with the rest of our team in Chicago—a man named Joe Ritchie and his son, Noah. Joe had lived in Afghanistan as a child and was now a multimillionaire. Both he and his brother, James, had appeared on the TV show *Sixty Minutes* the week before, telling about their incredible work in helping the people of Afghanistan. Joe would be a major part of my video assignment.

After a long flight with many connections, we arrived in Peshawar, Pakistan. A driver picked us up at the airport and sliced through traffic clogged with motorized rickshas, pedal bicycles, and kamikaze automobile drivers. A dreary, soupy cloud of car exhaust and floating dust particles hung in the air. No rain to speak of had fallen in the region for three years, which had turned the countryside into a chalky ecological disaster. Failing crops had devastated food distribution, and you could see hunger in the bland stares and bony cheekbones of the children. An odor of hideous soured smog filled our nostrils; the ever-present fumes burned our eyes.

We stayed in Pakistan for several days, maneuvering through endless meandering mazes of bureaucratic red tape to secure our visas to cross the border into Afghanistan. At last we received permission and immediately left Peshawar, driving up the treacherous mountain divide known as

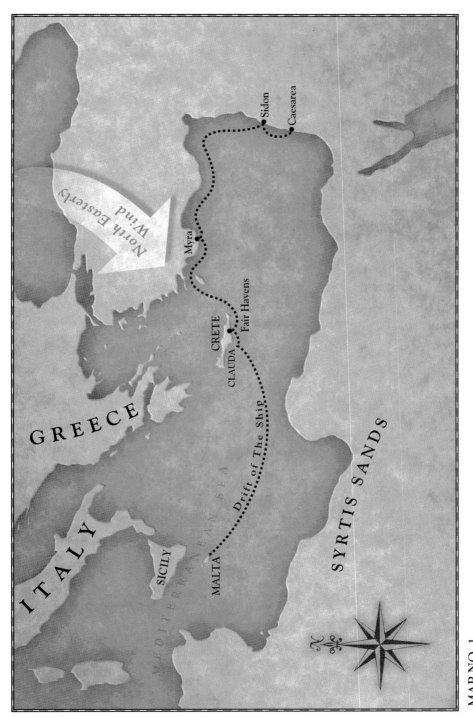

MAP NO. 1

MAP NO. 2

Inset map detail shown on MAP NO. 3

St. Paul's Bay

St. Thomas Bay Area

Marsaxlokk Bay

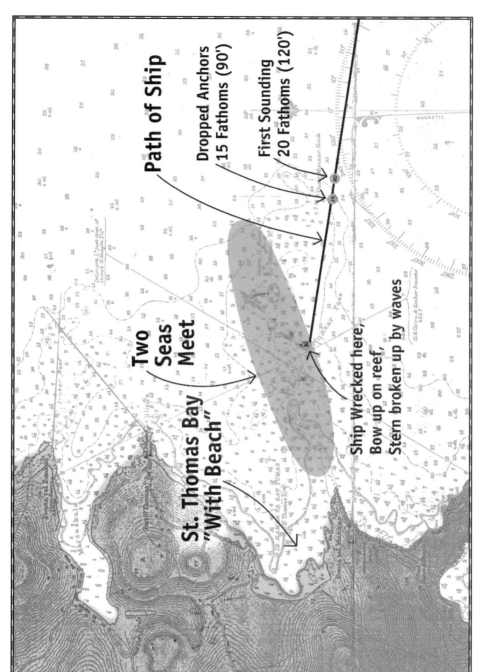

Path of Ship

Dropped Anchors
15 Fathoms (90')

First Sounding
20 Fathoms (120')

Two
Seas
Meet

St. Thomas Bay
"With Beach"

Ship Wrecked here,
Bow up on reef,
Stern broken up by waves

MAP NO. 3

3

One of the first dive canisters used by early divers on Malta

Wilfred Perotta (right) with Tony Micallef Borg
Tony was renowned as a great diver on Malta and
involved with bringing three of the anchors
from the Munxar Reef

Wilfred Perotta (left) with unknown dive companion displaying a pole of grouper from the
old days of spear fishermen. Circa 1960s

Author Robert Cornuke (left), Professor Bonanno, and Charles Grech kneel behind the anchor found by Tony and Charles in the early 70s on the Munxar Reef.

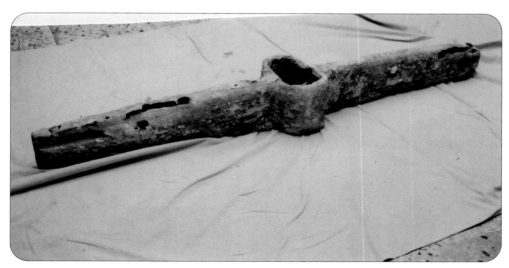

Anchor stock found by Ray and Tony in the early 70s on the Munxar Reef.

Lead dive weight from melted anchor stock found by Tony and Ray on the Munxar Reef in the early 70s. (Note the 'MT' chiseled on the face of the dive weight.)

Anchor stock found by "Mario" in the late 60s on the Munxar Reef.

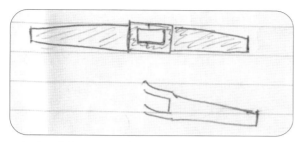

The hand sketch of cut/melted anchor by witness Charlie Vella.

Model of an ancient Roman/Alexandrian anchor. The wood would have decayed rapidly in the sea, but the lead cross piece known as the anchor stock would last indefinitely on the ocean floor.

Picture of Marsaxlokk Bay with traditional Maltese fishing boats called Luzzu.

Left to right: Angela Phillips, Dr. Mark Phillips, Dave Ladell, Jean Francois La'Archevec

Cliffs just north of St. Thomas Bay.

Bob Cornuke (left) with Jim Fitzgerald on a sandy beach of St. Thomas Bay. (Author believes this is the beach where St. Paul and surviving shipmates swam to shore following the shipwreck.)

This photo was taken during mild storm surf on the Munxar Reef "where two seas meet."

(Note: the currents come together on the reef from different directions.)

A reenactment of how Tony and Ray lifted the anchors from the sea using barrels filled with air.

St. Paul's Island, the island of legend where many say St. Paul's ship came to rest (the Bible says the ship of Paul was stuck on a **reef**). The geographical features found on St. Paul's Island do not match with the Biblical narrative.

BASE research team left to right: Jim Fitzgerald, Bryan Boorujy, Jerry Nordskog, Gail Nordskog, Jay Fitzgerald, Bob Cornuke, Yvonne Miles, Edgar Miles, David Stotts, Jeremy Miles (in back)

Wilfred Perotta with Ray Ardizzone holding the first dive tanks used in Malta.

Ray Ciancio, the protégé of Tony. When he was 14 years old he witnessed the discovery of two anchors found on the Munxar Reef.

Robert Cornuke (in the white shirt) in Afghanistan with pushtun body guards.

Author with Major Manuel Mallia inputting data into the computer to analyze direction of the drift of Paul's ship from Crete to Malta.

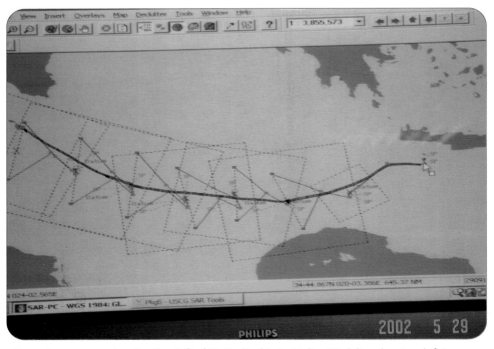

Computer program showing the drift of St. Paul's ship to Malta. (Dark line denotes drift.)

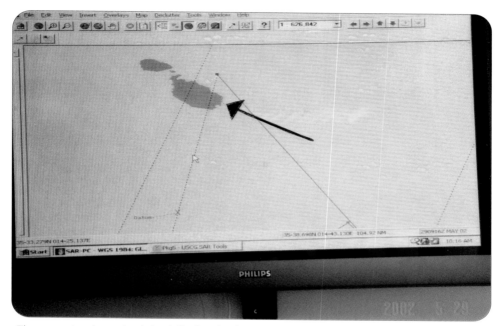

The computer determined the drift of Paul's ship coming from the south, encountering the island of Malta on the Southeast coast in the area of St. Thomas Bay.

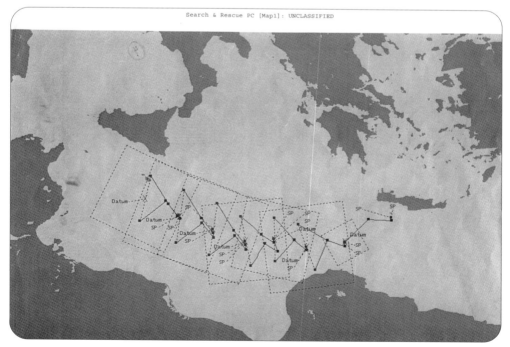

Computer findings on the drift of Paul's ship.

15

Lead sounding weight—a device used on ancient Roman vessels. The weight was tied to a rope and dropped into the sea to determine sea depth.

Just north of St. Thomas Bay, a freighter lies victim of a 'gregale' storm. The waves are crashing over 80 feet high.

Khyber Pass, across which invading armies have traveled for thousands of years. Upon arriving at the border crossing in Afghanistan, we were greeted by thousands of people walking, driving, limping on crutches, and being carried on litters—all desperately trying to escape Afghanistan. Swarms of disabled and homeless men, women, and children congregated at the border crossing, staring helplessly through barbed wire gates through which they would never be allowed to pass.

AFGHANISTAN—DECEMBER 2001

Descending from the Khyber Pass, we drove alongside a meandering camel caravan and entered the northeastern frontier of Afghanistan. Across this vast no-man's-land of lawless disorder, grief and graves were all that remained. Everyone, it seemed, carried some kind of a rifle, pistol, or grenade launcher. Small boys wore ammunition belts proudly strapped to their chests, and we could sense an almost overpowering cloud of oppression—it filled the air, clung to one's skin. Generations of death and war had choked all joy and hope from these people. Children played among the carcasses of tanks and armored vehicles that littered the landscape, and the barren, dust-caked hillsides lay pocked with moonlike craters, like a scene from Hades.

Within a few hours we had reached Jalalabad, which would serve as our home base during our stay. The smoky, dust-shrouded sunset brought a gloomy end to another day of historic suffering in Afghanistan. We spent the night in a mud-walled compound. Armed civilian soldiers passed by my window every few minutes, their slow-moving forms casting eerie shadows from the pale moonlight. My bed consisted of a blanket spread over a mat on the floor. A Kalashnikov AK-47 machine gun had been "lovingly" placed on my pillow, a gift from my Pushtun host.

The Pushtuns are mountain people, vast in number, comprising a major portion of Afghanistan's population. Since there are over sixty different tribes in the country, the Pushtuns are in constant struggle with one another for land and power; feuds between families are often passed down from generation to generation. Unwritten codes rule tribal conduct and include, among a host of bizarre social rituals, the protection of guests—and I was a guest of a Pushtun tribal leader named Nastrula.

Nastrula was a friend of Joe Ritchie, whose self-appointed mission was simply to help his people, by whatever means possible. He had worked on numerous relief-aid projects, some of which involved repairing parks and damaged irrigation systems traditionally used for the underground poppy trade. In Afghanistan, growing poppies had fueled a huge heroin trade, diverting critical agricultural irrigation and manpower from other, food producing crops. Joe was committed to helping Nastrula implement some sort of reform and redirection of these illicit activities toward "life-giving" agricultural projects. It was a terribly risky outreach, but I was impressed to see that Nastrula and Joe had made important inroads to help stem the region's deadly preoccupation.

The next day I would be traveling to Kabul to try and find the prison and the place where Dayna and Heather had left their journals. Nastrula assigned me two guards with machine guns and a van and driver for the long, bone-jarring journey. Before I left on my trip to Kabul, however, a war correspondent from the *Sunday Times of London* warned me that people were being attacked on the road to Kabul all the time.

"If you go to Kabul," he cautioned, "take no less that three trucks of armed guards."

When I told him I was going with only two guards and a van, he shrugged. "Well, then, you'll be my next story for the *Times.*"

It took five hot, jarring hours traveling through a swirling dust storm to reach the city of Kabul. More so than anywhere else we'd visited in Afghanistan, the landscape here was dominated by the remnants of war: Tanks, destroyed buildings, bombed-out neighborhoods filled the horizon as far as we could see. It was a scene that previously I had witnessed only on CNN; now I was now driving through the middle of it.

Night was falling by the time I arrived at the Kabul prison that had served as Heather and Dayna's temporary jail. It was really a "women's reform school" that had been used by the Taliban as a prison for women who were disobedient to their husbands, their fathers, or their faith. As Dayna and Heather had discovered, the slightest offense would land a woman in this cruel compound. In Afghanistan women could be beaten for simply wearing nail polish and could not work outside the home unescorted by a male family member. And under Taliban rule, if a taxi driver so much as drove a woman alone, he could be severely beaten for the offense.

So far I had encountered no resistance from the locals, which seemed somewhat odd. The United States military was currently pulverizing this country, cleansing it from the Taliban pestilence, and one would think an American civilian would attract unwelcome attention. To this point in the journey we had been spared, but as I strolled toward the front of the prison, a machine-gun-carrying bearded man walked over to me and stood with his arms crossed.

He introduced himself as a Northern Alliance commander and barked, "It will be impossible for you to enter today."

"All I want to do is take some film of the prison," I said, holding up my video camera.

"No! Forbidden!"

I had been in these situations before and had learned a few tricks. From my jacket pocket I removed a new watch, purchased for $6.95 at a Wal-Mart in Colorado. I pressed a button on the side, a pale green glow illuminating the dial. I placed the watch respectfully in his hand and said, "This watch is my gift to you."

He took the watch, looked around, and whispered, "This prison is my gift to you."

Within minutes I was videotaping Heather and Dayna's prison cell—a small, dirty room located off of a courtyard that was barren and dusty but for a lone tree in the middle. Heather and Dayna had faxed me a map they had sketched of the prison, and as I surveyed the scene, I knew I had found the right place.

Heather and Dayna told me as a way of identifying their cell that a woman in their group had mixed fingernail polish with mud and painted animal figures on the walls. Since the Taliban forbade paintings of any kind, the pictures had been whitewashed over, though one rough draw-ing of an elephant remained on the back wall. (Heather later told me that someone else probably sketched the elephant drawing after their escape.) The only thing that remained in their cell area was a blue strip of cloth stretched across the room to serve as a clothesline. I pulled down the blue cloth, rolled it up, and placed it in my pocket. Heather had said that every evening hundreds of flies perched on this blue cloth, offering the women a little "entertainment" during their imprisonment.

The next day I videotaped the home where the missionaries had lived prior to their arrest. Another commander in Kabul told me that the journals of the American women had been burned, so by noon the next day I left Kabul to return to Jalalabad.

As I drove through the Kabul Pass toward Jalalabad, my driver and guards pointed out men with guns on a ridge on the canyon walls. They then directed my attention to large dried bloodstains spread across the ground. "This is where, just one month ago, robbers robbed and then killed four journalists," my driver said. Gazing at the bloodstained rocks, the driver motioned discreetly toward the men on the cliffs, heads wrapped in turbans, rifles in hand.

"Al-Qaida," he whispered. "It is very dangerous for us. We must go now."

Paul's Endurance

The guns, the blood, the war, the maimed children, the insects, and the oppressing dust storms made for one of the most arduous trips I've ever been involved in. This was a foreboding land immersed in misery.

I thought, *How in the world did the apostle Paul do it?* Enduring year after years of lonely, dangerous travel into hostile, alien cities and lands. I had traveled a few thousand miles and had been away from home for two weeks, but it is estimated by some that Paul traveled over twenty thousand miles in his various journeys.[20] That's twenty thousand miles without planes, trains, or cars, every mile of it on foot, by hoofed transportation, or ancient ships. And, as he himself wrote,

> *...in labors more abundant, in stripes above measure,*
> *in prisons more frequently, in deaths often. From the*

Jews five times I received forty stripes minus one; three times I was beaten with rods; once I was stoned; three times I was shipwrecked; a night and a day I have been in the deep; in journeys often, in perils of waters, in perils of robbers, in perils of my own countrymen, in perils of the Gentiles, in perils of the city, in perils in the sea, in perils among false brethren; in weariness and toil, in sleeplessness often, in hunger and thirst, in fastings often, in cold and nakedness. (2 Corinthians 11:23–27)

Paul traveled thousands of miles, among warring tribal factions and dens of robbers. Through beatings, shipwrecks, and hardships, he traversed that brutal and unforgiving ancient world, enduring it all, every day, tirelessly spreading a message he knew to be true.

The man who once persecuted Christians was met on a roadway by his Lord and entrusted with a message that he would spread even in the face of death. He didn't stay in the confines of his protective group, but went out into a wild and dangerous world that wanted him dead.

Here in Afghanistan I could plainly see that, like Paul, Heather and Dayna had traveled a similar road. They had endured arrest, suffered persecution, and were even were spit on as they share their faith. There is always a price to pay when you take a stand for what you believe. Paul ultimately died for his allegiance. But, as that great apostle said, "For to me, to live is Christ, and to die is gain" (Philippians 1:21).

A person who converts from the Muslim to Christian faith in Afghanistan is considered dead by his or her family. He or she is severed from family ties, cut off socially. This social segregation for accepting an alternative to Islam prevents almost anyone from proclaiming a new faith of any kind. It's not surprising to me that today Afghanistan is estimated to be 99 percent Muslim.

Paul met with similar prospects in his efforts to share his faith. If someone from a Hebrew family accepted the Christian faith, that person was also considered dead by the family. But even in the face of constant persecution, Paul never stopped preaching the Word. He was relentless.

Traveling the dangerous back roads on our way back to Jalalabad, I couldn't help but think of Paul's commitment to his faith and his gutsy resolve. Feared, hated, beaten, robbed, spit on—nothing stopped him. In God's plan, nothing could.

ANCHORS OF HOPE

During my return flight to the United States, I mentally replayed my experiences in war-torn Afghanistan. I reached for my Bible to perhaps gain some perspective. I found myself journeying once again through the pages of Luke's narration and lingered over the words Paul penned from lonely outposts and prisons across the perilous ancient Mid-east. In my time on Malta, and now in the blood-soaked land of Afghanistan, I felt that I had met this man named Paul in a more personal way.

I discovered that this man who changed history's course was now changing mine.

The anchor I had touched on September 10, 2001, had suddenly become something more than mere lead. To me, the anchors had become a symbol of hope, a witness to one of the greatest stories ever told—of deliverance from death of those on Paul's ship who had lost all hope so long ago. As I stared out the window of the plane, my mind traveled back to the Munxar Reef and Malta's secretive fraternity of divers. If those anchors really were the anchors from Paul's ship, then those with no hope in their lives needed to know. With the death and devastation of Afghanistan now behind me, I felt more inspired than ever to continue the search. ⚓

Chapter Thirteen

THE MAN PAUL

*T*he fondest memories I recall from my youth in Southern California are those when I was sitting with my grandmother on her plastic-covered sofa, having her read to me from books about far off places. Grandma was an immigrant from Russia, and when reading, she slowly enunciated each word because of her thick Slavic accent. Despite no formal education, she would walk to the library every week, check out three or more books, carry them home, and read each one. As I quietly sat there, I listened to her read on and on, intently watching while she slowly turned each page with her frail, silk-skinned hands. With a stack of books, Grandma could carry me away to distant, exotic lands, setting my sails for a life of travel and adventure.

As I reread many of the books of the New Testament that the apostle Paul wrote, I realized that no one has ever come close to the experiences of Paul when it came to travel and adventure. Not only had he traveled most of the known world during his time——enduring deprivation and suffering hardships that would have caused even the boldest explorers to quit, Paul amazingly counted those brutal trials and travels as both an honor and a privilege. He forged ahead through beatings, hunger, imprisonment, even shipwreck, until, as he said himself, "His very life had been poured out like a goblet of wine."

A CITIZEN OF ROME

The Rome of Paul's day had overcome its ancient beginnings as a poor, obscure, small city-state east of the bend of the Tiber River to become the world's most powerful empire. The Romans were disciplined, hard-working builders of magnificent cities and colossal monuments, and a succession of visionary emperors acted on their insatiable need for power. Rome's military leaders were cunning in battle and strategic in their political alliances.

From beyond Rome's far frontiers, kings and ambassadors brought opulent gifts and tributes to placate the empire. They knew that to be allied with Rome meant safety and protection. A friend of Rome enjoyed extensive personal rights and privileges. An enemy of Rome typically faced death and destruction.

Paul was born a Roman citizen in Tarsus and educated by the Rabbi Gamaliel in Jerusalem. Paul came to hate Christians and persecuted them with a peculiar drive and zeal. On one occasion he held the garments of a mob stoning a follower of Christ, named Stephen. Paul feared the new cult of "believers" that had multiplied so quickly around the teachings of the so-called heretic Jesus, who had so blasphemously proclaimed Himself to be the Son of God and had been put to death on a cross. Jesus had spoken out against the hypocrisy, lies, and legalism of the Jewish Pharisees—a privileged class of rabbis and priests (of whom Paul had sacrificed all to become a distinguished member). Paul, in turn, became a relentless, self-appointed pursuer of any and all who held to this Jesus' radical teachings, presiding over the deaths and imprisonment of scores of Christians and contributing in no small part to the scattering of the early church. Little did he know that life as he knew it was about to end. Paul was about to go from the hater to the hated, from the hunter to the hunted.

Most of us have heard of Paul's dramatic conversion experience since we were children in Sunday school: Paul, en route to Damascus to arrest more followers of "The Way," encountered a flashing light brighter than the sun and fell to the ground blinded. From within the light he heard the voice of Jesus, the Messiah of Israel, asking, "Why are you persecuting Me?"—a short sentence that marked the start of the incredible ministry of one of the New Testament's great apostles. Within a short time this ruthless persecutor of the church had undergone an amazing transformation that baffled his allies, confused his enemies, and ultimately, changed the world forever.

At first the Christians feared Paul, unable to believe that their former jailer now preached Jesus as *Messiah*. His old cronies, the Jewish Pharisees, stamped him as a lunatic traitor to their faith. Much like Paul had been only months before, they could not stomach the fact that an executed criminal named Jesus could have so many followers so many years after his execution. And, then, in the type of inexplicable turnabout that made their blood boil, Paul himself, their lead persecutor, had converted too. It certainly filled them with a disgust that, on a smaller scale, exceeded their hatred of the Romans, who still occupied their land. No one could have confronted the depths of their religious hypocrisy like this formerly high-ranking Jew now preaching the new religion of the man whom he talked about as being the "Son of God." Plainly put, Paul had committed national treason because of his new belief, and the Pharisees vowed to get rid of him.

Their first opportunity arrived when Paul entered the Temple in Jerusalem after having publicly fraternized with unclean Gentiles. Upon hearing that Paul had entered the Temple compound with his "filthy" friends in tow, the Pharisees quickly formed a mob and descended on the Temple complex. Once inside, the angry throng grabbed Paul and dragged him out of the compound, beating him with the intent to kill. As news of the riot reached the Roman commander, he went with a company of soldiers to the angry crowd.

After quieting the riot, the Romans guards bound Paul in chains and took him to the barracks. The commander of the Roman forces in Judea saw no reason for a trial for this Jewish troublemaker: A riot had started in the streets of Jerusalem and Paul was clearly to blame. He would be beaten until he confessed, or died.

A soldier stood near Paul and tensed his grip around the whip, a menacing ensemble of leather thongs interwoven with jagged bits of metal and bone. But before the centurion could administer this patently Roman form of justice, Paul lifted his bloody face and sternly inquired, "Is it lawful for you to scourge a man who is a Roman and uncondemned?"

The soldier's outstretched arm dropped to his side, his whip dangling in the dirt. The centurion immediately went to the commander and told him that the Jewish prisoner has just claimed to be a citizen of Rome; and with that, Paul's destiny changed.

(For a Jew in Roman Judea, it was nothing unusual to be dragged to jail, accused of being suspicious, and then beaten into submission. But to flog a *citizen* of Rome, especially without a trial or legal condemnation, was strictly forbidden.)

The commander quickly came to Paul and asked, "Are you a Roman citizen?"

"Yes," Paul replied.

Shocked, the commander probed further to see if his prisoner was simply a wealthy Jew who had bribed his way to a privileged position.

"With a large sum I obtained this citizenship," the Commander said. (Obviously he wasn't born a Roman citizen.) Paul replied, "I was *born* a citizen."

Alarmed at realizing that he had put a Roman citizen in chains, the commander contemplated his next move and ordered Paul to be untied. The next morning, hoping to clear up what had become a confusing mess, the commander ordered all the chief priests and their council to appear before him. Minutes later Paul stood before the crowd to give an account of himself. "Men and brethren," he began, "I have lived in all good conscious before God until this day."

Even this basic claim so incensed the high priest that he ordered Paul hit about the mouth. Spitting blood, Paul shot back at them, saying in essence, "You hit me without charge, you hypocrite. You sit and judge me, and you strike me without being charged, so you're the one who breaks the law."

By meeting's end, another furious mob had tried to wring Paul's neck, and once again the soldiers had to drag him to safety. Paul was later ordered to appear in Rome and would continue to contend with brazen threats against his life—in one case narrowly escaping a clandestine plot by forty men bound with an oath to neither eat nor drink until Paul was dead.

Ultimately, two hundred soldiers, seventy horsemen, and two hundred spearmen accompanied Paul on his way to Caesarea, illustrating just how great a sensation this story had become in the middle of the first-century Roman world. Paul was big news, already renowned among believers in that region—many of whom believed that even handkerchiefs and garments Paul touched would heal the sick. And now his peculiar fame had spread across the empire, triggering deep, passionate emotions in everyone who heard his story.

In Caesarea, Paul fell under the jurisdiction of Felix, a former slave himself, who rose (with the help of some strategic marriages) to become Governor of Judea. A greedy man, Felix let his famous prisoner sit in jail, hoping to collect a substantial bribe, with the result that Paul languished in a prison for two more years.

"YOU ALMOST PERSUADE ME TO BECOME A CHRISTIAN."

Paul's fate would veer toward the island of Malta when Felix was replaced as governor by a fellow named Festus. Confronted with the same politically risky mess that Felix had faced, Festus tried to make it easy on himself. He simply asked Paul if he would be willing to be tried in Jerusalem.

Paul refused and demanded to make his appeal directly to Caesar.

In those days, every citizen of the Roman Empire had the right to appeal to Rome, or "Caesar's judgment seat." In Paul's case, it presented a dangerous logistical dilemma, for the prisoner would have to be transported all the way back to the city of Rome, where he would then be held until his case could be heard in the high court. But Festus apparently saw it as an easy out, for after hearing Paul's abbreviated defense and appeal to Caesar, he readily replied, "You have appealed to Caesar? To Caesar you shall go."

Confined to prison while waiting at Caesarea for his transfer to Rome, Paul had a unique opportunity to speak directly with King Agrippa II, who visited Caesarea to welcome Festus to his new post. Agrippa II was the grandson of the infamous Herod the Great, who had tried to kill the infant Messiah by slaughtering all the male children less than two years of age in the districts of Bethlehem. Herod's grandson apparently shared the same arrogant disregard for the God of the Jews that had motivated his demented grandfather. One writer described the Herod family tree as "infested...murder, maneuvers for power, incest, and moral dissoluteness marked its many branches preceding and during the incarnate and risen ministry of Jesus Christ."[21]

Yet Agrippa II took an unexpected personal liking to Paul. Though Festus had no way of knowing that Rome's ruler in Judea would take an interest in this lowly Jewish prisoner, he explained the chain of events that led to Paul's arrest and imprisonment. Festus must have been stunned when Agrippa quickly called for an impromptu hearing. We can only imagine the tension that must have been hanging in the air as Festus set up the assembly and then watched Agrippa and Bernice glide through the standing crowd to their royally appointed thrones. The regal pair no doubt looked around the room until all was perfectly silent, and once all eyes were on them, they took their seats.

With a wave of his hand, Festus ordered the chained prisoner brought before the assembly, detailing the strange sequence of events that brought Paul to Festus's court. Agrippa turned toward Paul and said, "You are permitted to speak for yourself" (Acts 26:1).

Here again, Paul's audience with the king demonstrated the persuasive power of the gospel. Paul's speech played to Agrippa's prior knowledge of all things Jewish—so much so, in fact, that by the end of his oratory, Festus had no better response than to issue a feeble insult to Paul's intelligence: "Paul," he cried, "you are beside yourself! Much learning is driving you mad!"

The place undoubtedly erupted in laughter.

As the uproar subsided, Paul's response must have drawn a collective gasp from the crowd for its brashness in the face of Roman might: "I am not mad, most noble Festus," Paul replied calmly, "but speak the words of truth and reason." He then appealed to what he knew of Agrippa's expertise in the Hebrew Scriptures and challenged it directly. Paul—the lowly Jewish prisoner, bruised and scarred, disheveled, and probably sick from two years of prison—stood bound in chains in front of the highest authority in Judea, then spoke one of the most courageous lines in all of courtroom history.

"King Agrippa," he said, "do you believe the prophets? I know you do believe." Paul spoke these brazen words to the highest authority in Judea, challenging the spiritual accountability of the king himself. The audience could scarcely believe the gall of the accused.

Even two thousand years later, it strikes us as a brilliant, disarming question. For if Agrippa indeed professed to believe in the prophets, he undoubtedly knew that Jesus fulfilled, in detail, exactly what the prophets wrote about Messiah in the Hebrew Scriptures. It also meant that Paul was innocent and should be released. However, if Agrippa said he didn't believe the prophets, he would offend the Jewish leaders, who took the writings of the prophets as the very Word of God. And if Agrippa offended the crowd, he could easily create a political mess, if not an outright revolt.

It was a no-win situation for the king. The prisoner had backed him into a corner with no way out. The best thing for Agrippa to do at that point was to laugh off the question altogether—so that is exactly what he did.

Agrippa looked straight at Paul and replied, "You almost persuade me to become a Christian."

Paul held up his chained arms and instantly replied, "That's what I am praying for...." With that, the king rose, along with Bernice, Festus, and those sitting with them. They briefly conferred in another room and agreed that Paul hadn't committed anything resembling a capital crime, or even anything deserving imprisonment.

"This man might have been set free, if he had not appealed to Caesar," said a confused King Agrippa.

But Paul knew that God wanted him in Rome, and he looked forward to the opportunity. No amount of hardship, imprisonment, torture, or personal danger would keep him from his final appointment. The wheels had been set into motion.

Paul, a lowly prisoner bound in chains and completely at the mercy of Rome, prepared to board a ship that would sail out on a journey toward the epicenter of the "civilized world." As he stood on the deck of a small Adramyttium ship and watched the harbor of Caesarea—with its gleaming breakwater and impressive, colossal statues, disappear into the watery horizon—Paul must have smiled to himself at God's amazing sovereignty. Here He was, using all the resources of Rome to move the message of Jesus the Messiah from Judea to the entire world. ⚓

Chapter Fourteen

A Third Anchor

*I*t had been little over a month since my return from Afghanistan when I got an excited call from my friend Ray in Malta. He was talking so fast, and with his thick Maltese accent, I almost couldn't understand what he was trying to say. But I did hear the words "third anchor."

"Third anchor?" I interrupted.

"Yes, Bob," he said, "There is a third anchor. I couldn't stop thinking about Tony and the other two anchors I told you about, so I did a little checking on my own. I asked the old group of divers, and several people remembered that an old diving buddy named Charles Grech had brought up an anchor from the Munxar. He brought it up with Tony shortly after we found the first two."

I hesitated a moment before asking, "Do you know where this Charles is?"

"Yes, yes," Ray said eagerly. "He owns a nice restaurant in St. Julian's. I went to see him, and he told me how he and Tony found an anchor while hunting lobster by The Bank on the Munxar. He said he found a lead anchor stock a little over five feet long, right in front of the big cave."

As Ray's excited stream of words began to slow, he added, "Bob, I would think that the only time you have three anchors together on the seafloor apart from a shipwreck is if somebody cut them away from a ship."

Typically, he explained, when an anchor is found on the sea bottom all by itself, it's the result of being snagged on a rock, like snagging a fishing line. When the anchor won't come free, it's cut.

"But *three* anchors, Bob, getting snagged at the same time, in the same place—this is hard to believe."

Ray had caught the excitement of the search for the anchors, and I could tell that he had been thinking about the proximity of the three anchors and what that meant. His logic seemed valid. And he noted something else: Solid lead anchors were extremely expensive in Roman times, just as they are now. There existed virtually no scenario in which someone, much less an experienced sea captain, would have just dropped three critically important, and *costly,* anchors and left them in the sea unless they had a mighty compelling reason. We had already explored what those reasons might be: (1) All three went down with a ship during a shipwreck—even though most shipwrecks are found on reefs or in shallower water, not in ninety feet of water as these three were reportedly found; or (2) these anchors were dropped from a ship on purpose.

On the long odds they had been dropped on purpose, it would be an unlikely coincidence, given what we already knew, for them to be found several centuries later—along the shoreline geography the Bible describes; in front of a bay with the same distinct features that the Bible lists; in the same depth of water that the Bible specifies; and of apparently the same vintage we would expect to find on a first-century Alexandrian ship like the Bible portrays. They also came to rest where "two seas meet," just as the Bible states.

Still, I had begun to ask myself what seemed to be a question crucial to determining whether these anchors had been intentionally cut loose or had gone down with a ship. If the anchors went down with a ship, for instance, then where were the *remains* of the ship? Had there been, or were there, legitimate remnants of a wreck, or a typical debris field one might expect of such an occurrence, somewhere beneath the sand near where the anchors once lay?

Entertaining the possibility that Ray, or one of the other Maltese divers, might turn up additional anchors, I had begun reading Lionel Casson's excellent book *Ships and Seafaring in Ancient Times*. In it he writes, "When an ancient vessel came to grief and landed on the seafloor, the movement of water and sand and the action of marine borers gradually destroyed the exposed parts of the hull and other elements made of organic matter...this is why no hulls of freighters carrying grain are ever found: grain was transported in bulk or in sacks, and if a ship loaded with it went to the bottom, the cargo soon vanished along with the hull."[22]

Based on this, I was fairly certain that, had a ship wrecked near the Munxar Reef, nothing of its hull or rigging would have remained after almost two thousand years. Yet other wrecks around Malta had yielded plenty of small debris: items such as clay amphorae or coins. The same would be true of the Roman freighter. I hoped to someday secure permission from the Maltese government (which is required) to search the seabed for additional clues. It would be interesting to investigate not only

165

the area around the Big Cave but also farther toward shore, at the base of the reef where the huge grain freighter would have gotten stuck and subsequently sunk.

Ray's phone call both stirred and encouraged me. The mounting evidence caused me to wonder: If Ray had located a third anchor, perhaps the fourth and final anchor could be found as well—either still concealed on the bottom of St. Thomas Bay, or perhaps in the hands of an unknown diver. In my optimism, I even went so far as to conjecture that some of the remaining lead weights from the melted first anchor might also be tracked down. And why not? Doors that had been locked shut for two millennia now seemed to be creaking open.

As I ended my phone conversation with Ray, I asked if he might ask Charles to send me a photo of the third anchor. Ray agreed to ask, though it seemed like a long shot. I literally could not believe my eyes when, a couple of days later, photos of a Roman anchor appeared on my computer screen in an e-mail from Charles. From what we had learned about ancient anchors, Charles's anchor definitely appeared to be a first-century Roman anchor stock. Suddenly Ray and his old diving club had warmed to my theory and were cheerfully serving as amateur sleuths helping me piece together a two-thousand-year-old puzzle.

Within a few days of receiving the e-mail and photos, I called Charles and asked him if he would allow a film crew to videotape his anchor. He said he would and commented, "I never would have thought that an old anchor would be of such interest to anybody."

He hadn't yet been made privy to the source of my keen interest in his "old anchor," so I explained to Charles my theory step-by-step, starting with Paul's voyage from Caesarea, to Sidon, to Myra, to Crete, toward the shore of Africa, then finally to a point intersecting Malta in the south, in St. Thomas Bay.

I waited for a response, but all I could hear was Charles's soft breathing over the phone. And then, quite pensively, he remarked, "I do not know if I believe all that is said in the Bible, all the legends and stories. But if this is proven to be from Paul's shipwreck, it will be history." He paused. "I will need to rethink some things about this book, the Bible."

I proposed that on my next trip to Malta, I could bring experts who could examine the anchor to certify its dating and authenticity. He thought about it for a few moments, and then finally echoed concerns similar to those I had heard repeatedly from Malta's early diving fraternity. He openly feared being hit with a heavy fine, or even prison, if his anchor indeed turned out to be an ancient historical artifact. As a diver, he well knew the laws governing the discovery and full disclosure of ancient objects collected from the seafloor.

I confessed that I had no easy answer for him about legal issues and conceded that he certainly might incur difficulties from the government of Malta. I had crossed this bridge with Tony's wife, Margaret, and I knew the problem had to be solved. If these people, because of my inquiry, found themselves trapped in a publicity storm for possibly possessing anchors from Paul's shipwreck, then all of Malta, maybe even the world, would be asking how such priceless artifacts came to be in the possession of a group of Maltese spear fishermen.

MALTA, MAY 23, 2002

It took me more than a month, but I finally cleared my schedule and pulled together a research and film team. I returned to Malta with Jim

Fitzgerald and his son Jay; friends Edgar and Yvonne Miles and their son Jeremy; Jerry and Gail Nordskog; videographers Bryan Boorujy and David Stotts; and my good friend Darrell Scott (Darrell's daughter Rachel was the first student killed at the Columbine High School tragedy in Littleton, Colorado). The night after our arrival, we were seated together in a seaside restaurant in an exclusive section of Malta's St. Julian district. Our host was the restaurant's proprietor, Charles Grech—owner of the third anchor.

Charles greeted us at the door with a huge smile and an ample girth rounded from years of sampling from his well-appointed kitchen. After customary introductions, the team sat down and menus were passed around. Charles said, "Let me, if I may, suggest your meal selections."

We enjoyed a wonderful dinner, and as the group finished their meals, Charles and I made our way to a quiet table on the terrace, overlooking the bay. Without any prompting, Charles started right in.

"Tony and I found our anchor on February 10, 1972. It was the Feast of St. Paul, the day we celebrate Paul's shipwreck on Malta. I remember that day too because it was my thirty-third birthday. I started diving when I was a young man." He laughed and patted his belly. "The fish were plentiful, tourists were hungry, and business was good. One day after I had been diving for fish, a man named Tony saw me tossing my fins and mask and other diving gear in my car. Divers were few on the island in those days, so when Tony saw me putting my gear in the car, he had to meet me."

Charles recalled that Tony was with his dive buddy Joe Navarro and that the three of them became fast friends and began diving together. Over time they pitched in to buy a few Aqua-Lungs and a German rubber dinghy with an eighteen-horsepower engine and started up a little company called CTJ—for Charles, Tony, and Joe.

"We spearfished together, sold the fish to the pubs and restaurants, and started some other small commercial ventures." He pointed to the bay. "Scraping the bottoms of boats, things like that. You know, anything to make money while diving."

All the divers I'd met on this island enjoyed reminiscing about the carefree old days of youth, but most of all they liked spinning tales of all the days they spent spearfishing with Tony. A young waiter stopped by our table. "Sorry to interrupt, Mr. Grech. Would you like anything more?"

Charles casually waved his hand and asked, "Anything for you, Bob?"

"No thank you, Charles," I said, eager to hear the rest of his story.

Charles ordered a cappuccino, then looked back at me in a contemplative manner. "This is my last night at the restaurant," he said. "I've sold the old place." He turned and looked at the moored fishing boats silhouetted in the moonlight in the dark harbor and sighed, "I'm now going to just fish. I like so much to fish."

It was clear that he was feeling wistful and nostalgic, but I couldn't help myself. I steered the conversation back to the anchor. "Tell me about the day you found the anchor with Tony," I said, overly impatient to hear his story.

"Well, Bob, there had been a big storm. Afterward Tony asked me to go catch lobster with him on the Munxar. It was hard going in Malta in those days, so we did anything to make a few extra pounds. Lobsters would get the best money, and the caves on Munxar had plenty.

"Well, we were diving out on the Munxar and pulling ourselves across the rock and groping in the holes for lobster." He demonstrated by thrusting his hands outward and back. "Then, there it was—this big anchor, slightly exposed through the sand. The storm probably agitated the ocean bottom, and the currents had shifted the sand to reveal a straight edge of lead. We brushed away the sand and saw just how big it was—over five feet long.

"Once we were on the surface," he continued, "Tony said that he had found other anchors at this very spot. He said we needed to go get some empty metal drums to bring the anchor up."

Charles told Tony that he had a powerful wench that could lift the anchor from the seafloor to his boat. Charles said they eventually took the barnacle-encrusted slab of lead to his own house, where the anchor began to reek in the afternoon heat. He moved it outside, and that is where it has remained to this day.

Then I heard something that was like receiving an electric shock. "There was another anchor found on the outer Munxar," Charles said, looking right at me with a locked-on stare. "The anchor," he continued, "was a big Roman achor just like mine. It was found by a man named Mario."

"A fourth anchor?!" I stammered. Excitement swirled with mental confusion. Could this really be true?

I had come a long way from being on my own shipwreck in Ethiopia to now possibly learning about a fourth and final anchor. Leaning forward with transparent eagerness, I said simply, "Charles, tell me about Mario."

Charles looked at me and saw a face that shared every bit of his own building excitement. "The day I heard about your theory, about anchors from St. Paul on the Munxar, I couldn't sleep," he said. "My mind would not rest. And then I remembered the time I found a small anchor, one that was less than two feet long, in shallow water. I brought it up, and while I was putting it into the trunk of my car, a fellow diver named Mario saw it. He laughed at how small my anchor was and asked me where I found it. I told him, and he said that he had found a large Roman stock on the Munxar, but it was much bigger than mine, over five feet long."

Charles shrugged his shoulders and laughed. "Why I remember such a short conversation from so many years ago, I don't know."

Sipping the last foam from his cappuccino, he stood up and placed his hand on my shoulder. "I don't know where this fourth anchor could be. I heard that Mario died several years ago. But I think I know of the village where he once lived. So if you want, tomorrow we can go out there and see if we can find out anything about him. If we cannot find Mario's anchor, we will still be able to see mine at my house."

Standing to shake Charles's hand, I said, "Thank you, Charles."

He was in high spirits and apparently confident. "We *will* find this fourth anchor," he said, smiling exuberantly. Then, exiting the terrace, he nudged me and pointed toward the dazzling moonlit bay. "And then we will do a little fishing!" ⚓

Chapter Fifteen

THE FOURTH ANCHOR

*E*arly the following morning, a soft rain fell from low misty clouds as we waited for Charles in the hotel lobby. Grumbling tourists had congregated around the windows, complaining about the gray soaking rain.

I paid no mind to the weather. I was anxious to get started looking for the mysterious Mario the diver of Charles's distant recollection. Shortly, Charles drove up in a white SUV, skidding to a stop on the wet driveway in front of the lobby entrance. I hopped into the car and we sped off. He seemed just as energized about our search this morning as he had been the night before.

"I did a bit of calling last night after you left," he said, wheeling the SUV out of the hotel parking lot. "I talked to an old friend who confirmed that Mario once lived in a village in the south part of Malta."

"Great, let's go!" I said, and for the next thirty minutes we swerved down a maze of narrow twisting roads, passing scooters and small cars, honking and splashing water in a tangled ballet of frenetic traffic.

We drove into a typical Maltese town with a large, Baroque-style domed church in the town's center. As we stopped and got out of the car, church bells chimed a progression of throaty *bongs,* filling the town square and beyond with a resonant, melodic hum.

I had noticed that every village in Malta revolves, in some degree or another, around churches like this one, their splendid domes dwarfing the cluster of surrounding villas and homes; their interiors adorned with gilded ceilings, ornate altars, and magnificent frescoes. Demographically speaking, about 87 percent of the people living in Malta attend church regularly, a higher percentage than in any other country in Europe. In the summer months, each church and village maintains a sort of rivalry with the other parishes, competing to see who can produce the most ornate festivals, parades, and fireworks displays.

"Where do we begin the search?" I asked Charles as he parked the car and we stepped out onto the street. We stood surrounded by a dense cluster of homes, roads, and shops.

Charles explained, "Families live in these villages five, six genera-tions, or more. People do not move around here like they do in America. Still, this may not be so easy because there are numerous Marios living in this area."

Even so, chances were slim that many of these local Marios had been accomplished divers from the old days.

Charles walked over to a street vendor selling his wares from a small stand next to the sidewalk, his cart bulging with melons, leeks, zucchini, squash, and onions. Thinking we might be interested in his produce, the roadside merchant held up two large squash for our inspection. Charles immediately began his inquiry about a man named Mario who was a diver thirty years ago. After a short conversation in Maltese punctuated by several quick exchanges of nodding and talking, the merchant motioned, using a squash as a pointer, toward a door directly behind us. We turned to see the entrance to an older quaint Mediterranean villa, constructed in traditional Maltese style: a pleasing, two-story facade abutting the narrow sidewalk running in front of a long row of buildings.

"Who lives here?" I asked Charles as we stepped up to the door.

Charles smiled broadly. "The man explained that this is where 'Mario the diver' lived—and that his widow still lives here today."

As I tried to fathom this seemingly unbelievable merging of chance and coincidence, Charles rang the doorbell. From the balcony above us, wooden shutters opened and a woman leaned over the railing. She shouted something to Charles in Maltese, and after a short, animated conversation, the woman disappeared and soon reappeared, opening the heavy front door. There, from a thin gap in the doorway, she continued her lively dialogue with Charles in English (I assumed Charles had told her I was an American).

"Hello," she said. "Can I help you?"

Charles smiled politely and replied, "I was one of Mario's good friends many years ago. You and I were once at a wedding together."

"Oh yes, yes," she said with a look of doubtful recognition. I took her to be Mario's wife, or a close relative—a sister perhaps. As the conversation progressed, she nudged the door open wider.

"I'm sorry for the way I must look," she said, patting her hair with an air of embarrassment. "I was not expecting visitors today."

Charles said, "We have something very important to ask you." Justifiably confused by our sudden appearance at her doorstep, she seemed a bit puzzled but nonetheless swayed by the urgency in Charles's voice. Opening the door the rest of the way, she waved us into her entry hall and pointed to a side parlor.

"Please come in and be seated. I will be with you in a moment."

She disappeared up the stairs, leaving us in a room decorated with antique pots, old nautical maps, and ancient treasures. Within five minutes she reappeared, smoothing her dress and patting her freshly brushed hair. Seating herself in an antique wooden chair directly in front of us, she took a deep breath and said, "I can listen to you now. Please go on."

"I was sorry to hear about Mario," Charles said.

So she was Mario's wife.

"He died twenty years ago," the woman responded with a pained smile. She tilted her head, reminded of the memory, and sadly raised her eyebrows.

Glancing my way, Charles explained to her, "This is Bob Cornuke, from America. He is here in Malta researching an ancient shipwreck—a very important old shipwreck."

The woman (she later asked that she and her husband remain anonymous, so I have changed his name) turned to me and asked, "Did Mario have something to do with the shipwreck you are speaking about?"

I measured my words, realizing I stood in the presence of perhaps the only person alive who could direct us to the fourth and final anchor. "He may have," I replied slowly. "Do you know if Mario ever spoke of bringing up a large Roman-style anchor from the seafloor?"

"Yes," she answered, "I know that Mario brought up such an anchor. I think it was in the late sixties, but I can't be sure about that."

I swallowed. "Do you know what he did with this anchor?"

"Yes."

Expecting her to elaborate, I hesitated a moment and then asked, "Does this anchor exist *today* in Malta?"

"Yes," she replied again, without emotion.

"Do you know where it is?"

"Yes."

I took a deep breath. Did I dare ask her the next logical question, knowing her answer held enormous implications for our entire mission? I paused a moment and decided to forge ahead. "Can you show us that anchor?"

Standing up from her chair, Mario's widow invited us through a doorway into the bright sunshine. We rose to follow her outside, where sporadic raindrops fell from a few remaining scraps of cloud, yielding patches of brilliant blue sky. She motioned to a short wall in the courtyard, and there, resting in front of her garden, lay a huge Roman anchor stock.

She didn't seem to grasp the magnitude of what she possessed, but said simply, "It is too big to keep in the house." For several moments the three of us stood staring at the precious lead treasure. Charles wore a glazed look of stunned amazement, muttering below his breath, "It looks just like my anchor...the same size, the same color." He jerked around to look me in the eye. "This could be *my* anchor, Bob. It is my anchor's...*twin.*"

The stock was a long, rectangular solid lead casting rendered in the identical Roman/Alexandrian motif as the others. It had the telltale square center hole, which once held a huge wooden shaft; the two arms together spanned over five feet, radiating out from the hollow square center. Neither arm was perfectly straight; each had a slight bow in the lead.

Kneeling down, I ran my hand over its wet, barnacle encrusted side. It was cool to the touch. Then I steadied myself and strained against its

177

bulk to test its weight, but I couldn't even budge it. Before me sat a massive monolith, stone cold and immovable, whose size, weight, and potential biblical significance struck me with awe.

I stood up and asked, "Do you know where Mario found this anchor?"

"I remember Mario saying that he found the anchor on the Munxar," she said, "or maybe on the island of Camino. Mario was one of the first divers in Malta, and he found many objects in the sea. But as far as this anchor, I am not sure where my husband found it. I only remember him saying something about the Munxar or Camino." She closed her eyes for a moment, dredging her memory, but looked up and said, "I'm sorry that I can't be more specific for you."

I could see that she badly wanted to tell me exactly where her husband had found this anchor, but too much time had passed and nothing was left of the distant conversation she had had with him about his find.

Still, I needed to be certain about this anchor. As incredible as the anchor was, its origin remained a mystery. All I knew for sure was the woman's vague "it may have come from here or there." *Had it come from the Munxar as had the other three?* The chances seemed fairly bright: If two of the three other anchors had survived intact almost two thousand years, then the fourth anchor could have lasted until now as well.

Or had this anchor been lost to the seafloor during some other ship's misfortune on the unforgiving rocks around Malta? Maybe it had snagged on the sea bottom and had been cut loose by another huge ship somewhere on the island of Camino, far removed from the Munxar Reef. Or, just maybe, it was indeed the fourth anchor we were looking for.

Standing in the garden, I stared silently at the anchor at my feet, wishing it could speak. I didn't know, in that moment, where I might find the answers to the questions that raced through my brain. But experience had taught me that somewhere, somehow, *someone* knew where Mario had found this anchor. ⚓

Chapter Sixteen

THE WINDS OF FATE

he excitement of the past two days—meeting Charles, tracking down Mario the diver's widow, and locating the possible fourth anchor—had distracted me from the very thing I had come to Malta to do. I still hadn't seen the anchor Charles said he had raised from the Munxar Reef in 1972. As anxious as I was to see it, I didn't want to do so without the benefit of Professor Anthony Bonanno's expert opinion. On a prior trip, Malta Professor Bonanno (head of the Department of Archeology at the University of Malta) had graciously viewed video clips of Tony Micallef-Borg's anchor (chapter 10). If anyone could verify the authenticity and dating of Roman anchors, it would be Professor Bonanno.

The morning after visiting with the widow of Mario the diver and seeing what we hoped might be anchor four, I met up with Professor Bonanno and the rest of the research team and drove to Charles's home to see his alleged Roman anchor. (Perhaps prematurely, we had already taken to calling it "the third anchor.")

We met Charles at his house and made introductions all around, then waited as he excused himself to retrieve the anchor. After a few minutes he reappeared, straining to push a wheeled dolly on which sat a huge lead anchor stock—a mirror image of the stock we had seen the day before in the garden of Mario's widow. We rushed over to help him move the anchor out where we could see it in the sunlight.

With all of us struggling to maneuver the dolly outside, I asked Charles, "How in the world did you get this thing onto the dolly?"

He laughed. "It took *five* of us—four young men plus myself—to even lift it."

As Professor Bonanno began to examine the anchor, our entire team wrestled it off the dolly so he could get a better look. Even with several full-grown men pushing and heaving, it barely moved. *How in the world,* I thought, *could anyone retrieve this metal monster out of the sea?*

Finally Professor Bonanno knelt down and placed his hand on it.

"Where was *this* anchor found?" he asked, looking around at the group.

Charles stepped forward and said, "A man named Tony and I found this anchor thirty years ago. It was sitting on the seafloor, where I have now heard that two other anchors, and possibly a fourth, were also found."

Turning his gaze back to the anchor, Professor Bonanno inquired, "Four anchors at the *same location?*"

"Yes," said Charles. "They were brought up from the Munxar Reef off St. Thomas Bay."

Bending down, Professor Bonanno took the next several minutes to examine the anchor up close, from every conceivable angle. Finally he stood up to address us as a group, his tone and demeanor deadpan and professorial, as though he was teaching in his classroom at the University.

"What I am looking at is clearly a solid lead anchor stock, a stock of a Roman anchor," he explained. "A Roman anchor consisted mostly of a wooden structure, with two lead parts. The most important part was the lead upper bracket, which is called the 'anchor stock.' This object here is a typical Roman anchor stock. The wooden stem would have come out of this square hole in the center. It bends on one side in one direction and on the opposite side in a different direction in order to allow the anchor to grip the seabed. The lead anchor stock is what you find in the sea because the wooden parts usually rot away."

He turned and glanced again at the ancient object and then said matter-of-factly, "This type of anchor would have been quite common during the period from the first century B.C. to the first century A.D. If one finds marks on an anchor stock, one can be even more specific. Sometimes they will have the name of the owner of the ship, allowing one to identify the owner and perhaps trace to specific dates. I have tried to look for special marks that might permit us to date this stock more exactly, but I don't see any in this state of preservation. Perhaps when one removes the encrustation we may find identifying marks."

I asked the professor whether or not he felt that this anchor stock was consistent with the type of anchor that could be aboard an Alexandrian grain freighter such as the one that carried the apostle Paul to Malta.

I felt my jaw tighten, and the professor continued. "It could have belonged to a cargo ship, possibly a grain cargo ship, and possibly one from Alexandria. Such ships used to ply the Mediterranean from Alexandria to Rome." He rubbed his eyes as though searching his memory. "Egypt was one of the granaries of Rome, and we know from sources that occasionally such ships did stop at Malta. We know of two cases where Alexandrian ships came to Malta; both are described in the Bible. One of the ships, of course, was the ship that wrecked with St. Paul onboard.

Paul stayed on the island of Malta for three months; then another Alexandrian ship took him on to Rome."

As we absorbed his analysis, Professor Bonanno slapped his hands together, shaking loose some residue from the anchor's encrusted surface. Then he turned to me and said without emotion or inflection, "This anchor stock would fit very well within the era of St. Paul."

I took my small video camera out of my bag, opened the viewing screen, and showed Professor Bonanno video clips of the other anchor stocks (Ray and Tony's anchor, and Mario's). After watching video of both anchors, Professor Bonanno said, "From what I can tell from these videos —again without the benefit of physical examination—these other two anchors also appear to be typical Roman anchor stocks, appropriate to the era of St. Paul's shipwreck in Malta."

THE DRIFT

That night, I was notified that a high-level military official had granted us a rare opportunity. Amazingly, we had been given permission to have access to, and use of, a very expensive and sophisticated computer program that was being used by the Rescue Coordination Center of the Armed Forces of Malta.

This was both exciting and providential because this multimillion-dollar computer program had the high-tech ability to determine the drift of Paul's ship across the Mediterranean. Twenty-first-century technology was about to bridge an ancient gulf of uncertainty. The computer would objectively speak to us across the millennia and trace the, until now, uncertain path of the biblical event of Paul's journey from Crete to Malta. We would soon learn with reasonable certainty the uncharted course Paul and his fellow shipmates took in that terror-filled tempest over nineteen hundred years ago.

The next day we met with Major Manuel Mallia at the Headquarters of the Armed Forces of Wartime. Major Mallia was in charge of Air and Maritime Operations. He explained that we were at the Operations Center of the Armed Forces of Malta, which serves, among other things, as the Search and Rescue Coordination Center for Malta. The scope of their responsibility was revealed by his statement, "Our search and rescue region encompasses approximately a quarter of a million square kilometers, servicing a vast portion of the entire Mediterranean Sea."

I surveyed the operations center. Several men stood intently monitoring consoles, navigational charts, plasma-screen TVs, and radar screens, which lined the walls. Had this high-tech rescue center existed nearly two thousand years ago, these men would have received a distress call from the Roman freighter upon which Paul sailed. In response, they would have dispatched helicopters and sea rescue vessels, all the while listening to the frantic cries of the captain ordering equipment overboard and cables run beneath the ship to keep the swells from pounding the craft to pieces.

I had read of other disastrous shipwrecks in that era, when mishaps at sea were an all too common occurrence. In one account, the ancient historian Synesius described the following terror:

> The men groaned, the women shrieked, everybody
> called upon God, cried aloud, remembered their dear
> ones.... I noticed that the soldiers had all drawn their
> swords. I asked why and learned that they preferred to

belch up their souls to the open air, on deck, rather than gurgle them up to the sea.... Then someone called out that all who had any gold should hang it around their neck. Those who had did so, both gold and anything else of the value of gold. The women not only put on their jewelry but handed out pieces of string to any who needed them. This is a time-honoured practice, and the reason for it is this: you must provide the corpse of someone lost at sea with the money to pay for a funeral so that whoever recovers it, profiting by it, won't mind giving it a little attention....[23]

Even Josephus, the renowned historian of the first century A.D., endured a similar ordeal at sea. He wrote:

Accordingly I came to Rome, though it were through a great number of hazards, by sea; for, as our ship sank in the Adriatic [Mediterranean] Sea, we that were in it, being about six hundred in number, swam for our lives all the night; when, upon the first appearance of the day, and upon our sight of a ship of Cyrene, I and some others, eighty in all, by God's providence, survived....[24]

Standing in the Search and Rescue Center, I had to wonder how they would have handled such situations in ancient times: like the swamping of Josephus's ship, or of Paul's running aground on their island. As I admired the wealth of sophisticated equipment, Major Mallia informed me that he could use the Center's Search and Rescue computer system to model the precise circumstances leading up to Paul's shipwreck.

"This morning we are using our software to calculate drift against time of a hypothetical search object—in this case, the object will be the Alexandrian freighter that carried St. Paul. We define the known parameters, then input the appropriate data, such as the approximate size of the vessel, the days at sea, and the weather conditions as defined in the Bible. The computer will then calculate the probable drift of our search object."

He had my full attention. "Can you explain to me how it works?" I asked.

"Let's say you drop a corked bottle with a message in it off the coast of Crete. The computer can process the weather patterns during that time period, the currents of the ocean, the weight and drag coefficient of the bottle, and then calculate where that object would be in a day, two days, three days, and so on, depending on the given data.

"It is no different with a ship," he added with a shrug. "If we take a ship that was in a gregale and start it at a given point, we can calculate where it would go. The computer possesses millions of calculations on existing sea currents in the Mediterranean and has proven quite accurate in determining weather patterns, especially those weather patterns from annual storm systems."

The major explained that northeasters are most common in the Mediterranean and that the rescue center has amassed massive volumes of data pertaining to weather characteristics during these types of storm occurrences. The major walked us over to a console containing a large computer screen.

"What we will do," he explained, "is ask the computer to find a large wooden vessel meeting the general parameters of a grain freighter from the time of Paul. We can even input the type of hull—its *wood type*—and then take into account the veering characteristics of a northeaster, adding to it the leeway of time and the history of currents during the fall season when this incident would have occurred."

Staring into the screen, the major said softly, "We will start the computer program after I input all the pertinent data."

With my Bible open, I explained where the ship of Paul had been traveling at the time the storm blew it off course.

"The ship was going from a port called Fair Havens," I began, "traveling along the southern coast of Crete, going in a westerly direction. The Bible says that a 'favorable south wind' occurred, suggesting that the ship was probably going around the Cape Matala when it was suddenly slammed hard by a northeaster, today referred to as a gregale." I told him that the last known coordinate of Paul's ship came off of the southern coast of the small island of Clauda, where in a desperate attempt to save the ship, the sailors pulled the skiff onboard and undergirded the ship with cables.

As we began to input the data, an alarm suddenly sounded over the loudspeakers, indicating that one of the center's many daily rescues was commencing. The major turned to me casually and said, "We have an incident. We can no longer continue the computer program. I'm sorry, but if you could return tomorrow, we will finish then."

As we hastily gathered our gear to leave, the big flat-screen TV mounted in the search operations center showed a live black-and-white video feed of helicopters circling a stricken vessel in the middle of the Mediterranean. The dilapidated vessel was being tossed about in huge swells and fierce wind some two hundred miles off the coast of Malta.

Before we left the Search and Rescue Center, the major stopped me and said, "You know, our tradition on Malta says that Paul's ship ended up in St. Paul's Bay." Then he smiled. "Tomorrow the computer will answer the question of the direction in which Paul drifted in the storm the Bible describes."

THE DEFINING MOMENT

The next day we returned to the center. It was a beautiful day, the wind calm and the sea relatively smooth and flat. Upon entering Major Mallia's office, we were greeted with a warm reassurance: "The weather looks okay until later in the afternoon, when the wind picks up and the seas get rough."

We returned to the sophisticated array of equipment, which Major Mallia proudly announced had been donated by the United States Coast Guard following an extensive bilateral training course. The major explained that the new Operations Center in which we were sitting was only three weeks old. The room, in fact, smelled of new paint, rubber, and plastic.

It felt to me like a defining moment. Much was at stake for me personally. The equation was simple: If the computer determined a northerly drift, it would *eliminate* my primary search site. If, however, it calculated a southerly drift, the helplessly drifting ship would have impacted the southeast coast of Malta, aligning perfectly with the Munxar Reef theory. Depending on the outcome, this exercise could also put in grave question the possibility that Paul's ship ever could have landed anywhere on the northern coast of Malta—more specifically, the traditional site of St. Paul's Bay.

The major began to input the data directly out of the Bible and then simulated a northeasterly storm system as described in the Book of Acts.

"Now we will see," he said, turning to me. "Each quadrant in our computation comprises a forty-eight-hour period of drift. The massive amount of data takes some time to compute. It is, however, as accurate as we can possibly get."

Our team crowded around the major's chair to watch. A version of history never before seen now unfolded before us. As the first forty-eight hours of drift appeared on the screen, it showed Paul's ship traveling in a westerly direction from the lee of the tiny island of Clauda. At that point, it looked like it would be a coin toss whether it would then go north or south. However, as the next forty-eight hours began to plot on the screen, it showed Paul's ship veering sharply to the south in a steady, wind-driven drift. The next several quadrants of the program, in fact, showed the ship missing the northern coast of Africa by as little as seventy-eight miles. No wonder the sailors aboard Paul's ship were so frightened! To strike and shipwreck on that coastline would have been certain disaster. Without water available to them for hundreds of miles, they would have been overtaken by thirst and succumbed to a miserable death.

To explain why the ship didn't strike the African coastline, some Bible translations describe a sort of drag mechanism being deployed at or near this junction, in the ship's out-of-control movement. More than likely, a sheet of sail in the shape of a windsock was used to slow the ship's rate of progress and artificially steer it back out to sea. The text in its original Greek literally says that the sailors "let down [from above] the vessel, and in this way were driven." Interestingly, this same type of emergency sea anchor/parachute is still used by sailors today in catastrophic storms.

The computer labored on according to the raw data, its soft-glowing screen flickering digital updates of the route taken by Paul's ship as it was driven by the storm. Major Mallia kept looking back at me as the process unfolded and muttering, "This is surprising to me. Very… *surprising*." Staring into the screen, he had become totally focused on the events playing out before him. Finally, whispering to himself, he said, "This computer is quite accurate. The conditions we have inputted are as close as we can assess the conditions at the time of Paul." Then he took a slow, deep breath and said, "I never could have imagined that the vessel's drift would come…from the *south* as you had surmised."

Over the next half hour, the computer continued to generate forty-eight-hour quadrants, ultimately showing the ship intersecting Malta. Turning toward the major, I asked, "Precisely where would Paul's ship have been at the end of fourteen days?"

He looked back at the screen and then down at his data files. "The computer shows the object striking Malta sometime in the late evening or the early morning hours of the fourteenth day."

Acts 27:27 tells us, "On the *fourteenth* night we were still being driven across the Adriatic Sea, when about midnight the sailors sensed they were approaching land."

With my heart rate increasing, I then asked, "Where does the drift show the object hitting Malta?"

Very slowly, very deliberately, the major said, "This dotted line is within the area where we would expect the drift object to be. *Anywhere* on that line." Tracing a finger across the screen, he said, "…that line hits Malta on the *south,* where we also find the Munxar Reef."

Neither of us, or any member of our team, could find words to express the significance of the computer's findings. As we slowly allowed the major's words to settle in our minds, he softly and deliberately confirmed our theory.

"The spine of the Munxar Reef is shallow, going perpendicular to the land, more than a mile off shore. In a storm like the one described in the Bible, it would be treacherous. Knowing the way heavy, steel-plated ships can be wrecked on it, I hate to imagine what would happen to a wooden ship colliding with the jagged stony jaws of the Munxar Reef. There's no way any ancient ship could have survived." Then, as if thinking aloud, he recalled, "Behind the Munxar Reef is a sandy beach, and the currents in a storm system as described in the Bible would eventually wash anything wrecked on the reef onto that beach."

Finally, unable to ignore the pregnant silence, the major turned, looked me in the eye, and said simply, *"It is surprising even to me!"*

Everyone in the Search and Rescue Area stood in stunned silence, staring at the computer screen. After the initial excitement of watching the arc of the ship cross the computer screen, the final verdict struck me as neither somber nor exciting.

As in other investigations I had undertaken around the world, the converging pieces of the puzzle amid the longest odds brought only a feeling of thankful relief. I knew that, while even such a sophisticated software program can be fallible, what stood before us is the best available technology to realistically model what happened to Paul's ship.

The computer program confirmed that the ship must have had come from the south and that its drift had completely eliminated St. Paul's Bay and other bays closely associated with it as the possible landing site. That left only two realistic candidates as the ship's possible landfall: St. Thomas Bay or Marsaxlokk Bay. Of these two, even Major Mallia agreed that only St. Thomas Bay possessed all the physical, nautical, and geographical conditions that aligned perfectly with the Bible's description.

ANOTHER SHIP MAYBE?

Even though the evidence was mounting that the anchors from the Munxar were from the ship of Paul, I had to consider the fact that another ship totally unrelated to Paul's might have sunk at the exact same spot. But given maritime logic, that notion seemed beyond the scope of probability.

The captain of Paul's ship had arrived off the coast of Malta, drifting out of control in the dead of night. The crew heard waves crashing in the darkness somewhere off the bow. The captain then quickly ordered the sailors to determine the depth of the sea by dropping a lead weight attached to a rope into the water. When he found out that the seafloor was receding in depth, he ordered four huge lead anchors cast in the sea from the stern. He did not have the benefit of choosing the best place to anchor on the coastline. In fact, when morning arrived, he learned that he had anchored at an extremely perilous spot. Would a seasoned sea captain choose to anchor directly in front of a reef being pounded by surf? He wouldn't have.

Could another ship with anchors from the era of Paul sink where the anchors were found on the Munxar? Most likely not. Close to shore, a ship almost always sinks from hitting rocks or a reef. The keel depth of a large wooden ship would not be able to hit the rocks ninety feet down, which is the depth that the Munxar anchors were found. Those anchors that were found thirty-five years ago by young Maltese divers on the outer Munxar were sent to the bottom by men who dropped them from a ship—not from a ship that sank.

Often in this type of investigation, gaping holes remain that need to be addressed, things that cannot, from all available evidence, be explained. But that didn't seem to be the case in this investigation. We not only had three, possibly four, of the anchors dated to the time of Paul; we also had computerized verification of the Munxar Reef's statistical probability as the shipwreck site.

Other critical details lined up as well: The anchors had been found in the approximate depth of water of which the Bible speaks; they struck bottom where "two seas meet"; and finally, they came to rest at a spot between the reef and the shore—a reef that would have been at a depth to allow Paul's ship to run aground and get the bow stuck and the stern submerged. Then, of course, there was a bay with a beach. No other possible place on Malta fit all of these criteria.

The exciting theory was now fusing with the reality of mounting coincidence. Several months prior, I had corresponded with Dr. Chuck Missler and posed the very question of the mathematical probabilities of another ship in history encountering all the unique circumstances of the Munxar Reef scenario intersecting with the biblical narrative.

Chuck Missler, a Ph.D., has had a thirty-year career developing high technology enterprises and has also served as a senior analyst for think tanks in the intelligence community. He would offer a unique perspective on the mathematical calculation of probability on the Munxar Reef findings as it relates to Luke's description from the Bible. Dr. Missler computed all the historical criteria of Paul's shipwreck, including drift direction, geological conditions, and the distinctive descriptions such as where "two seas meet," sea depth, the typology of the anchors, etc. His opinion was as follows:

Any attempt to estimate the a priori mathematical composite probabilities of encountering all the unique concatenation of the specific details you describe in relation to the Biblical text would clearly exceed the threshold of absurdity. (In mathematical physics, the threshold of absurdity, as required for the integration of asymptotic function, is defined as a probability of less than 10^{-50}. In the case of anchors, the inferred composite probability easily exceeds this, even without an application of Bayes' Theorem, etc.)

I asked Dr. Missler to put his opinion in simpler terms. His response was, "If you have four anchors, in the specific place you described, with all the specific criteria, then this is Paul's shipwreck."

The fourth anchor was now becoming all too important. Was it really a brother of the other three, or had it been found on some other reef and was therefore totally unrelated to our scenario?

It would have been easy enough to adopt a best-case scenario and call it good, but that would have thereafter left an open question. I had to keep working until I knew for sure about the mysterious fourth anchor.

WALKING IN ANCIENT ROME

On my last day in Malta on this third trip, I found myself strolling the lot that served as a set for the movie *The Gladiator*—an expensive, elaborate façade built to create a world of cinematic illusion. On the big screen, the set conjured up the sweeping splendor of imperial Rome; up close, it was little more than a hollow mask of wood, paint, and fading plaster.

Slowly making my way down a vacant Roman street lined with propped-up plywood walls, I pictured the set teeming with actors and cameramen. Now the only thing that moved was a piece of loose canvas flapping in the arid afternoon breeze. Exploring these modern-day ruins, I saw again how cruel time is to the worlds we construct for ourselves. Monuments fall, buildings crumble, and kings and emperors who once inspired fear are now so many specks of decaying dust—all the might that was once unrivaled Rome now reduced to crumbling columns and museum trinkets.

Along for the tour was an American film team headed by my good friend Jim Fitzgerald, who had come to Malta scouting locations for a video documentary about Paul's lost shipwreck. Lagging far behind the group, I found myself in an eerie moment of silent reflection, struggling to envision the Rome that Paul had encountered as a prisoner more than nineteen centuries ago.

Stranded on Malta for three months after the shipwreck, Paul sailed once more for Rome as a prisoner aboard yet another Alexandrian grain freighter, this one having wintered on Malta. Arriving finally in Rome, Paul must have gazed up at the imposing buildings as he was led through the city center. The Rome of Paul's day was of a scale and grandeur seen nowhere else in the world.

The streets would have been filled with throngs of people, noisy animals, and rattling carts—a bustling ethnic blend of freemen, slaves, citizens, emperors, aristocrats, and politicians. The citizens of Rome had an undisguised arrogance, deeming themselves civilized, merciful, and pious. Of course their enemies rarely lived long enough to offer an opposing opinion. Romans boasted of their civility, yet savored the sight of blood. Beast and man fought to the death in great public spec-tacles routinely staged in Rome's finest arenas. Once, history reveals, Caesar Augustus staged a gladiator show featuring ten thousand men; on another occasion, 260 lions and thirty-six crocodiles died to satisfy the bloodlust of the Roman population.[25]

Hardly intimidated by the spectacle buzzing around him, Paul knew that God had a high calling in store for him in Rome; he took courage in the fact his life lay not in Caesar's hands, but in God's alone. He may have been a prisoner in chains, but several months before, in the stillness of the Antonia Tower, Paul had heard the voice of Jesus in the Roman barracks in Jerusalem: "You have witnessed for me in Jerusalem; you must witness for Me in Rome."

Paul had no particular wish, desire, or plan to venture to Rome; he did so at his Lord's good pleasure. Ironically, his all-expense-paid trip to Rome occupied a rather obscure moment in history, yet the ember he ignited upon the spiritual deadwood of an unbelieving world still burns today.

The Bible provides us with only fifteen verses about Paul's visit to Rome. Oddly, once Paul arrived in Rome, there are no more Scriptures reporting stirring sermons or court dissertations; no more riots, no more mobs, no more beatings. Rather, Luke records that Paul was grant-ed the privilege of a private residence and a soldier to guard him. In the course of his stay, Paul summoned the Jewish leaders to his house, and when the curious crowd arrived, they were kept there from morning until evening as Paul spoke about his Lord and Savior. At the end of that long day of listening to Paul share the Good News, some were persuaded by what they heard, while some disbelieved, arguing amongst them-selves as they left.

So when they did not agree among themselves, they departed after Paul had said one word: "The Holy Spirit spoke rightly through Isaiah the prophet to our fathers, saying, 'Go to this people and say: "Hearing you will hear, and shall not understand; and seeing you will see, and not perceive.""' (Acts 28:25–26)

Then, as today, some people simply would not see, hear, understand, or perceive. I knew that, as with other biblical discoveries, even empirical evidence from the paradigm of history would fail to convince some skeptics. To these, the only evidence that matters is the court of public opinion, which says, under no circumstances can the Bible, much less Jesus' own claims or Paul's compelling testimony, ever be true.

I knew that when we presented the anchor story to the world, many would simply discount it. I understand this. It is predictable. But like Paul on his final mission trip, we have been granted a privilege of discovery that we are now compelled to present at face value. From here, people must make up their own minds. The experience of Paul and the other apostles demonstrated that, always, some will believe and some will not.

It is in Rome that the story of Acts ends. Paul remained under house arrest for two more years, though the rest of his life became something of a mystery. Today we are uncertain as to what specific circumstances ensued and are left to piece together a picture from fragments of second-, third-, and fourth-hand writings about him. A probable scenario has Paul being released from house arrest in about 63 A.D., from which he more than likely visited Spain and the area of the Aegean. From the Letter of Clement (95 A.D.), the Muratorian Canon (170 A.D.)

and the apocryphal Acts of Peter (200 A.D.),[26] we can reasonably surmise that, shortly thereafter, he was rearrested and put to death at the hand of Nero in about 67 A.D.

So it was that this shipwreck—this odyssey in chains across the Mediterranean, through a monstrous storm, and onto the rocks of southeast Malta—claimed just one chapter in a chain of life-shaping events the Lord ordered for Paul. Surviving a shipwreck and spending the winter on Malta filled but a short interval as Paul completed his ministry and faced his own death.

In my unexpected search for four lost sea anchors, I had been irreversibly swept up in the panorama of one man's complete commitment to Christ—a life so completely surrendered to his calling that he could write, at a time before his execution,

> *For I am already being poured out as a drink offering, and the time of my departure is at hand. I have fought the good fight, I have finished the race, I have kept the faith. Finally, there is laid up for me the crown of righteousness, which the Lord, the righteous Judge, will give to me on that Day, and not to me only but also to all who have loved His appearing.* (2 Timothy 4:6–8)

To some, the journey of Paul is good fodder for an inspirational sermon on Sunday morning or encouragement in times of severe trial. To skeptics, the account is one among a dusty compilation of old stories, little more than myth and legend relegated to the heap of endless literary fantasies.

To me, the account in Acts of the shipwreck of Paul became nothing less than an eyewitness account from a chronically accurate historian named Luke. And through my encounter with Paul's shipwreck and the artifacts of history—and, ultimately, with the man himself—I sensed I would never be the same.

I heard the group hollering for me in the distance. Their work at the set was done, so I made my way back to the van and we returned to the hotel. In the months ahead I would wonder about the anchor found by Mario the diver. Was this the fourth anchor, or was it brought up some other place? Was it the last piece of the puzzle that I was looking for? Or was it lost at sea by some other ancient vessel, only to be found by Mario somewhere known only to him? Would its original whereabouts be hidden from me forever?

Chapter Seventeen

GRANDFATHER OF MALTA DIVERS

MALTA—NOVEMBER 3, 2002

*I*t took me another six months to plan my fourth trip to Malta. The unsolved mystery of the so-called fourth anchor had, during the interim, kept me awake nights, dangling like a loose thread in the investigation. Leaving Malta the last time, I had been able to confirm eyewitness testimony linking the first three anchors to the Munxar Reef. All we knew for certain about the critical fourth anchor, however, was that it had been discovered by Mario the diver *somewhere* in the waters off Malta.

Interestingly enough, upon arriving back in Malta again, the rain was falling, just like my first trip, which seemed remarkable for an island with such a traditionally arid climate. The long hot days of summer had passed, and now a fall storm was drenching the almost deserted beaches and outdoor cafés. The tourists, it seemed, had gone home to Europe to toil in their jobs through the cold, damp winter, working to pay for next summer's warm Maltese holiday.

Meeting me at the airport was my good friend Ray Ardizzone, a familiar face from many of my prior expeditions. He was the one who led the prayer before our last-minute rescue on stormy Lake Tana two years earlier. That shipwreck in Ethiopia was the epiphany that launched me on this quest to begin with. Ray had been a faithful confidant and counselor, so it was appropriate that he accompany me on this last leg to track down the certainty of the fourth anchor being a brother of the other three.

Only weeks earlier I had received a phone call from Charles Grech (the man who found the third anchor with Tony), alerting me of rumors he'd heard from other divers on the island that a man named Wilfred Perotta knew where the fourth anchor had been found.

The first thing I did on landing in Malta was to contact the local police authorities and ask them for help in obtaining the phone number of one Wilfred Perotta. Wasting no time, I called the number and Wilfred answered the phone. I briefly explained my interest in finding information about Mario the diver and told him a bit about my theory on Paul's anchors. Wilfred replied with a simple, "Why not?" He invited me to come to his home to discuss the matter. One day later, Ray and I found ourselves shaking hands with this man who we hoped might know the secrets surrounding the fourth anchor.

At sixty-five years young, Wilfred's grip felt like a vise. Simply to look at him, one could see that he was a man of incredible physical condition, still working the piers, diving beneath ships, doing repairs and maintenance. On the island, Wilfred had long been known as the grandfather of all divers, one of the first three men ever to dive in the waters of Malta using oxygen canisters. At one time, like Tony, he was the underwater spearfishing champion of Malta. Walking through Wilfred's house was like entering an exotic museum, filled in no small part by his numerous diving trophies, which he proudly showed me. In 1960 he became the first athlete to win the sportsman of the year award on Malta, having participated in five world underwater spearfishing championships. A year before that, in 1959, he established a record, which will probably never be broken, during the world underwater spearfishing championship held in Malta. As impossible at it sounds, Wilfred speared six fish with just one shot.

His house was stuffed with artifacts that had been harvested from the sea. Thousands of unique seashells lined the walls, and diving gear from the pioneering days of scuba diving were all around. On his living room coffee table sat stacks of scrapbooks filled with fading photos and press clippings, even one showing a proud Wilfred receiving an award from Jacques Cousteau. Flipping open one of the many scrapbooks, I noticed that the pictures were invariably of Wilfred standing, speargun in hand, with several of his diving companions, mounds of fish at their feet.

Pausing at a picture of himself posing over a particularly large grouper, Wilfred laughed. "Today when someone finds a grouper that is three kilos, they claim it is a *big* fish. But we speared forty-kilo grouper many times."

On another page were pictures of Wilfred in various settings with Mario the diver. I saw a shadow of sadness sweep over his face as he remarked, "Mario was a good friend. We dove together all the time." He paused. "Mario died twenty years ago. We shared many good memories."

I didn't mean to be blunt, but I had to ask. "Did Mario ever tell you about an anchor he found on the Munxar?"

"Yes," he said, seeming not the least bit surprised by my question. "He told me that he brought it up with some other divers. I can't remember who they were. But I do remember Mario telling me that he hoisted up a massive anchor from out on the Munxar some time in the late sixties."

"Do you know exactly where he would have been on the Munxar?" I asked.

"He liked to dive twenty to thirty meters in depth—that's where the big groupers are on the Munxar," he explained. "That is probably where it was brought up, but we don't know for certain. The only thing for absolute certain is that he told me that he was out on the outer Munxar Reef when he found the large anchor."

I asked him if he had ever seen this Roman anchor. He told me that he had. "It's now at the home of Mario's widow, in the courtyard area," he said. That was the moment that I knew it: We now had four anchors from the Munxar location—four large anchors that appear to be consistent with the era of Paul's shipwreck.

Before I could ask another question, Wilfred stood up, turned on his television set, and slid in a videotape for me to watch. He had shot a spool of eight-millimeter film of those early days on Malta, when he was a young man, and had recently converted it to videotape. Even though I had at least a dozen more questions to ask about the fourth anchor, I relented to Wilfred's desire to share a chapter from his youth, sat back, and enjoyed the show. Over the next half hour, he took me on a sentimental journey of the diving lifestyle that he, Ray, Tony, and all the others had so loved and apparently still longed for.

"These are the earliest images of underwater diving in Malta we know of," he remarked, as the scratchy frames started flashing in the darkened room.

Watching the rare video, I became perplexed. "Wilfred, how in the world did you get film in 1956?" I asked, knowing they didn't have underwater cameras available to the public at that time. "And even if underwater cameras were available, how could you afford one?"

"Simple," he said. "I took an old watertight fuse box about eight inches by four inches by four inches and used it as a housing unit for one of the first underwater cameras. The fuse box had a small watertight glass plate on the front, and I placed my eight-millimeter windup camera inside."

As Wilfred narrated the flickering eight-millimeter film, he reminisced about the high-spirited, carefree days of Malta's diving pioneers. The homemade movie revealed in raw detail a brotherhood of young, athletic divers who reveled in the camaraderie and sport of their newly adopted vocation. Loaded down with primitive diving gear and rudimentary spearguns, Wilfred and his friends chased and speared trophy-sized groupers, brought them topside, and eventually strung the fish from a heavy wooden pole that sagged under the weight of the catch.

I had heard so many dramatic stories of these daring cowboy divers, but Wilfred's video finally gave life to the violent underwater reality of what hunting groupers, Maltese style, entailed. I watched, fascinated, as the divers used their intimate knowledge of the sea to lure these giant groupers out of the caves and then shoot them point-blank, holding on for dear life as the huge fish thrashed and tore against the implanted barbs. "The fish were so plentiful back then," Wilfred explained. "These island boys had been used to fishing with nets from boats, when suddenly they had scuba gear to take them into the groupers' natural environment." Malta's government eventually had to outlaw spearfishing altogether because the groupers became endangered. Wilfred stuck out in a few of the scenes shot by his diver friends, his trademark goatee dark and close-cropped, rather than the bib of gray now framing his chin.

After the video flickered to an end, Wilfred turned off the television and repeated the island's seemingly universal refrain: "You know," he said, "I've lost eight friends in diving accidents over the years." He set the video carefully back in its place and shrugged. "But enough of that," he concluded. "Let me show you some of the treasures I have in my home."

Wilfred's hundred-year-old villa doubled as an archival museum of scuba diving history unlike anything I'd seen in private or public hands. Literally thousands of seaborne artifacts, shells, and bits of diving equipment from his lengthy career sat perched on shelves attached to the patina walls of his home. Among the thousands of samples of undersea flora and fauna I admired were some of the earliest pieces of diving apparatus ever manufactured and used anywhere in the world. I walked past relics of hardhat sponge diving, weathered nautical charts, and bleached shark jaws lined with gleaming teeth. For a moment, I felt as if I'd stepped into a scene from Quint's boathouse in the movie *Jaws*.

When it came to diving, Wilfred had distinguished himself among Malta's diving elite as a brilliant innovator. He showed me, with pride in his eyes, one of the first diving masks ever used in Malta, which he himself created from two strips of an automotive inner tube and a pane of glass. He showed me diving tanks he had fashioned from cylinders scavenged from WWII airplanes and pointed out the first commercially manufactured equipment ever brought to Malta—a 1950s vintage Cousteau Ganon demand valve regulator and Siebe Gorman twin cylinders.

As we continued on, Wilfred disseminated so many facts on such an array of arcane nautical information that my mind could scarcely absorb it. Yet I stopped dead in my tracks when Wilfred offered, almost as an aside, "You know, along with those four anchors you've identified on the Munxar, I've heard of two more taken from shallow waters on the inner reef of the Munxar."

His words struck me like a lightning bolt.

A seemingly innocent remark could well deal a deathblow to a theory I'd spent two years developing. Wilfred seemed surprised when my jaw dropped and I stood staring at the floor. I didn't need to be reminded: The Bible specifically describes *four* anchors being dropped from the stern of Paul's ship. Nowhere does the Bible say "five," or "six," or "three." *Four anchors* were dropped from the stern of Paul's ship off the coast of Malta all those years ago.

MORE ANCHORS?

From the first moment, many years ago, when my personal experience taught me that the Bible was a more reliable guide to ancient sites and events than any commentary, atlas, or scholar, God's Word has never let me down. Our research team at the BASE Institute has inevitably found that the best answers to questions of history and archaeology—to say nothing of the issues of life—are found in the pages of Scripture. We have, in fact, been both startled and amazed at how clear, how specific, and how accurate the ancient Hebrew and Greek texts are in describing places, events, and other biblical details that have been inadvertently scrambled by translators and commentators over the years. I knew that, inevitably, the Bible would hold the key to this quandary and that this rumor of two additional anchors would stand or fall with Luke's painstakingly detailed account in Acts 27.

Ray and I discussed the issue at length that night, going over the verses in the Bible, and as I had suspected, the answer lay right in front of our noses all along. Even though the Greek New Testament words for bow and stern are similar, in revisiting the narrative, it became clear that there were certainly more than four anchors aboard Paul's ship.

We had already established that in the teeth of the storm the sailors had dropped four anchors from the stern, or the back of the ship...in *ninety feet* of water. And they dropped them while still some distance from the churning reef that they could hear surging in the darkness, in hopes of keeping the ship from smashing into the rocks.

But then we inspected the following verse, which states that immediately afterward, a small band of sailors, fearing for their lives, pretended to lower "some anchors" from the bow, or the front of the ship. Of course that was it! It hadn't occurred to me before, but there were other anchors onboard the ship in addition to the four they had already let down in the sea.

> *Then fearing lest we should have fallen upon rocks, they*
> *cast four anchors out of the stern, and wished for the*
> *day. And as the sailors were seeking to escape from the*
> *ship, when they had let down the skiff into the sea,*
> *under pretense of putting out* anchors *from the prow....*
> (Acts 27:29–30)

There it was again. When the sailors sought to escape from the ship, they did so under the pretense of lowering "anchors from the prow" of the ship, thinking they could get away with lowering the skiff instead. Paul foiled their plan, though, so they remained on the ship and eventually everyone survived.

We went back over the verses to make sure we hadn't misinterpreted the meaning. Since the word *anchors* here is plural (referencing the anchors in the bow), there had to be the prospect of putting out at least *two more* anchors—possibly more—from the bow of the ship. These would be in addition to the four already deployed and holding the ship off the rocks. And, as it turns out, the ancient Roman freighters carried *many* anchors. They were, in fact, the most important gear onboard— and they were invariably stowed in the bow. Given the dire nature of their predicament, if the sailors meant to flee the ship, pretending to drop anchors from the bow would be a logical, albeit deceitful, move. And when their plan didn't work...

> ...*the soldiers cut away the ropes of the skiff and let it fall off.* (Acts 27:32)

Now we had to ask ourselves: *Did they manage to drop the anchors into water? Were they in the skiff when it was cut away?* It's impossible to tell, but the word for *pretense* here seems to indicate a totally false motive—the anchors were nothing more than a ruse. The sailors' sole objective was to escape certain death by setting out in the small skiff— not to drop the forward positioned anchors. It's likely that the sailors never even touched the anchors in their escape plot.

This nugget of information had yielded two important new clues: First, the Bible indicates that the four anchors put off the back of the ship were the only four dropped at the fifteen-fathom (or ninety-foot) depth that Luke specified. Second, simple logic dictates that if there had, indeed, been other anchors onboard, they would be found in much shallower water closer to the beach, near where the ship actually struck the reef and went down.

The Munxar Reef trailed out to sea a mile and a half. The four anchors were dropped at the outer tip of the reef and the ship then sailed toward the bay, but they first had to go through the waves crashing over the Munxar. In other words, one could reasonably expect to find *at least* two additional Roman-style anchors (stored in the bow) in much shallower water closer to shore, *between* where the four anchors were deployed and the fatal reef that ultimately shredded and sank the ship.

These two new anchors mentioned by Wilfred should, in fact, have come to rest in a larger debris field, alongside an array of artifacts consistent with a 60 A.D. shipwreck. It all seemed to make sense on paper, but confirming such a scenario would require more time, more investigation, and more interviews. In some ways it felt like starting over.

Little did I know, within two days my answer would mysteriously appear.

Two nights after meeting Wilfred in his home, he called me at my hotel with a curious request. "Bob, I was so captivated by your explanation about why you feel Paul's shipwreck was on the Munxar Reef that I had to call you. I've been diving these waters for over forty years. I know every rock, every current, and every weather pattern. I also know every wreck site, and no one has ever found four anchors dating from the same era at any spot on Malta. Oh, there have been other anchors found, but not at the depths the Bible says and certainly not four together.

"Also, when you read me the verse in the Bible where it says the ship ran aground where two seas meet, it caused me to think and think about what you said. The two seas could only mean the Munxar Reef, because it is there that two currents come together and collide over the reef during a storm."

Wilfred was telling me nothing new. It was a description of the Munxar that had been corroborated in more than twenty interviews. I'd seen it myself: The currents come together over the Munxar. Even though I hadn't seen the waves on the Munxar in a big storm, I'd heard from many of the islanders about the waves on the Munxar creating a surging wall of water extending for more than a mile and a half out to sea. The phenomenon is well-known to divers and fishermen alike. More importantly, their descriptions fit perfectly with Luke's account in Acts 27:41.

Wilfred continued, "I was so intrigued with your theory that I decided to do some snooping around on my own. I talked with several among the small community of old divers on Malta and asked them about the four anchors at your site in the deeper waters of the outer Munxar. They know of the four you speak of, but…" he paused, "as I told you, there's one man who actually found two additional anchors in the shallows on the inner Munxar."

I waited as he cleared his throat and groped for words to explain his phone call.

"I have spoken with this man personally," he continued, "and…he surprised me when he said he wanted to meet with you. These men, these old divers, as you know by now, are a very secretive group. They do not share information easily. But when I told him about your theories, Bob, he said he had a personal reason why he wanted to meet with you."

I listened silently, trying to anticipate where this conversation was

211

headed when Wilfred added, "He does not want to be known. In fact, he wants to meet at an unnamed location. He knows he may go to jail or have a big fine for what he is about to tell you, Bob. He wants to meet tonight, and he wants to tell you of his two anchors he found on the inner Munxar."

Wilfred instructed me to go to the Black Pearl restaurant at 7 P.M. and wait in the parking lot. I agreed and found myself waiting beneath an underhang by the ship docks next to the Black Pearl. The fall evening had turned dark by seven, and the streets were filled with rain from a storm still blowing across the island. I saw Wilfred driving up on a small vintage European scooter. He stopped the scooter in front of me and said, "Get on." I had just left a meeting and was wearing a suit and tie. I must have looked quite a sight, sitting on the back of the scooter, speeding off into the wet night. I had no idea where we were going, and Wilfred seemed cautious, looking behind us on several occasions (I assumed to see if we were being followed).

We pulled up next to a bar that appeared to be closed for the evening. The sign over the door read "The Lucky Bar." Wilfred stopped the motorcycle, and a man wearing a plaid jacket stepped out of the shadows. He approached Wilfred with a swinging limp, and without saying a word, motioned for us to walk across the street to a small coffeehouse.

Once seated in the corner of the coffeehouse, the man quickly lit a cigarette and told me up-front that he didn't want his identity ever made known and demanded assurance that I would never reveal his name. After I agreed, he told the following story:

"Eight years ago I was diving on the Munxar Reef, spearfishing, when a fish darted underneath a rock. I looked under the rock, but I couldn't see the fish. I became frustrated. The fish swam underneath the small outcropping, but I couldn't see it. So I toppled over this rock, wanting only to satisfy my curiosity as to what had happened to the fish."

He talked slowly, seeming to visualize the entire affair in his mind. "I soon forgot about where it had gone, when I saw the straight edge of a large flat form covered in crustaceans. I unsheathed the knife from my leg, scraped the object, and saw the glint of metal. I had heard of other divers finding anchors, about their excitement at that moment, but it was the only anchor I had ever seen in the water. My heart nearly leapt out of my throat when I realized I had actually found a large ancient anchor."

I wanted to know more details—where exactly he had discovered the anchor, how he had brought it to shore—but he stopped me in midsentence.

"I am going to tell you that I found this and another anchor nearby." He paused. "It was also found on the inner Munxar in about ten meters (thirty feet) of water."

I pulled a nautical map from my pocket and asked him to pinpoint the exact location.

"It was eight years ago," he said, "but I know it was definitely in the inner part of the Munxar."

The place he pointed to on the map lay about two hundred or three hundred feet from the spot where I had earlier estimated Paul's ship crashed on the reef. From the site where the four anchors were cut loose on the outer Munxar, it sat a little over three thousand feet in toward the shore in a direct line on the inner reef. Most importantly, he said he found the two anchors at the shallow break in the Munxar Reef, known today as the Munxar Pass. This "pass" would have been the ship's only chance of survival in its desperate attempt to make it to the bay, which was just beyond the inner reef. So it made sense that the sailors would have tried to sail to shore through the small slit in the reef.

His story squared with the rough calculations Ray and I had made two nights earlier. I listened in earnest as the man told me he had heard from Wilfred of my speaking in churches about the Bible; he said he had come offering the information solely to assist in my efforts to tell the whole story.

"When Wilfred told me about all of your research, and how the Munxar lay where the two seas meet," he continued softly, "I couldn't help thinking how all those scholars, all those experts, deciding years ago that the shipwreck occurred in St. Paul's Bay. And they were wrong. I believe you have found the true location of the shipwreck of Paul. I don't know if what I'm telling you will help you or not, but I'm giving you this information, wanting nothing in return." He paused a moment, then added, "I am a religious man, I go to Mass, and I felt I needed to tell you so you could write in your book and speak to many people about the truth of Paul's shipwreck."

"Where are those two anchors today?" I asked, thinking there might be a remote chance of actually seeing the anchors and dating them to the same Roman epoch as the other four.

"I have children," he said, as he bowed his head in a somewhat embarrassed manner. "I sold the anchors for money. I am not proud of this, but this is the way of it. Life is expensive these days, and the fish…a lot of them are gone. It's hard to make a living." The man turned and nodded toward Wilfred, then rose from the table. Our brief meeting was already over. He had told me everything he knew, and it clearly fit the biblical narrative. We shook hands and he left as he had come, walking down the dark street, wet with rain.

Later that evening, as I reflected on our conversation, I replayed in my mind Luke's detailed description of two separate but connected incidents involving the ship's anchors. When the crew had dropped the four anchors from the stern, putting a hard brake on the ship's irresistible crash course toward the reef, another group of frightened sailors had perpetuated their own panicked intrigue. In their failed attempt to flee from the ship, they pretended to lower the forward bow anchors; instead, they ended up casting the lifeboat out to sea.

I found it astonishing that Paul, a prisoner onboard, discerned everything and exposed the crew's plot to the centurion, warning him that, "Unless these men stay in the ship, you cannot be saved." He knew that every sailor would be required to steer that big ship through the treacherous waters where the two seas met if they had any chance of reaching the safety of the bay.

And we all know the rest of story: The ship perished in the violent waves on the reef; the entire crew swam to shore safely; Paul and Luke went on to spread the Good News to a waiting world; and the anchors found their grave in the sand and rocks on the outer waters and the shallows of the inner Munxar Reef, lost to history for more than nineteen centuries.

My purpose here had ended as well. I had followed the trail of the anchors to its outermost reaches; and they, in turn, had spoken to me in soft, whispered secrets from the deep. All that remained was to say thank you to a new family of friends, bid farewell to exquisite Malta, and return home. ⚓

Chapter Eighteen

THE ANCHOR
OF OUR HOPE

*O*n my final day in Malta, I walked out to the edge of the sheer cliffs above the Munxar Reef. Standing there, I stared at the foaming waves breaking upon the rocks below. The storm during the past week had stirred the sea into mounting swells that were now merging together over the reef. The waves were fairly modest, nothing like you would see in a northeaster, where huge waves crash together sending plumes of spray forty or more feet into the air. The currents that carried these swells on their long journey to the southeast shore of Malta arrived from different directions, peeling upon themselves, offering a perfect portrait of what the Bible describes as "a place where two seas meet."

As I watched the waves swell and melt away, I reflected on my long journey's end. I thought of strong, big-hearted Tony diving down on this reef, to his "Bank," where the big groupers lay. My thoughts traveled to the unique fraternity of divers I met on my several trips to Malta and their colorful stories recalling the thrilling moment when the anchors pulled free from the grip of the seafloor and rose to the surface in a swirl of sand and excitement. I also thought of the apostle Paul and his exhausted fellow shipmates, clawing their way to the sandy shore below me. Sitting there, I wondered… *What* other *clues might still be hidden in the shroud of sand below the churning currents at the place where "two seas meet?"*

When I started the Malta project, I thought it would be a simple process: Go to the place Luke describes in the Bible, hire a boat, dive down, find the anchors, and then bring them up. I would follow an old storm that spoke a lost message written on the waves of time and the ancient pages of the Bible. I hoped that the Mediterranean had kept these anchors hidden for almost two thousand years under a protective canopy of sea. Ninety feet below, they would quietly wait for me to come along and wake them from their long slumber.

But, more than three decades before I started my search, several young Maltese spear fishermen got there first. With rubber and glass masks on their faces and metal cylinders of compressed air lashed to their backs, they dove down into the clear blue sea, discovering an archaeological find that I believe is of monumental importance. There, stuck in the sand, in front of St. Thomas Bay out on the Munxar reef, lay a cluster of huge lead Roman anchor stocks in a tangle of swaying seaweed.

These divers, however, didn't even consider that those artifacts could have been from the lost ship of Paul. The legend of Paul shipwrecking in St. Paul's Bay had existed for so long that it was indelibly etched in the Maltese culture, and consequently, anchors produced from any other bay could not be seen as being from Paul's ship. According to the long-standing tradition, Paul's ship went down in St.

Paul's Bay, and no other bay was even considered by those that discovered these ancient lead treasures.

By the time I arrived in Malta, the anchors were gone, removed from their sandy graves by young men who didn't even know the significance of what they had found. I consider it a blessing, however, that I wasn't the one to dive down and discover those anchors lying on the seafloor. Circumstances shielded me from the temptation of saying "I discovered." I did not pull anything from the sea and now can only point to the incredible accuracy of Luke's narrative and say, "These are the facts and they all line up."

For me, that is the greatest discovery I could ever hope to make.

Standing alone on the cliffs overlooking St. Thomas Bay, I wondered, *Why did Paul and the rest of those men on that Alexandrian grain freighter have to endure such incredible hardship? Didn't Jesus Himself tell Paul in a vision just prior to the voyage, "You must go to Rome"?* Certainly God, who controls all things, could have prevented that storm and calmed the seas; He could have made sweet, warm winds that would nudge the ship to Rome.

What was the meaning of that storm, of that frightful shipwreck?

Suddenly it occurred to me—the prisoners who survived that shipwreck, and who drew strength from Paul's heroic words, would go on to tell this miraculous story to other prisoners they encountered. The ship's owner, witness to the miracle of his own salvation at sea, would relate the tale to the aristocracy of Rome. The sailors would travel on to distant lands, everywhere speaking of their deliverance and of the Jewish slave who spoke to angels and served this man called Jesus. The soldiers no doubt carried the Good News of Christ down the long dusty roads leading to military campaigns in far-off frontiers. Through a terrible storm, from the ruins of a shipwreck, Paul's story would be carried on the lips of seafaring travelers the world over.

We have often thought of Paul as a solitary messenger chosen by the Lord to battle against all odds and fulfill the task of spreading the Gospel. But in the vast, unknowable economy of God, it had been ordained that *many* would carry the message of hope abroad. Through this humble story, I pray that the message about our one true Anchor—the Person of our eternal hope—will resonate once again across the globe, from a certain island called Malta. ⚓

AFTERWORD

$\mathcal{T}$he anchor stocks described in this book are prized by the families who inherited them from the sea. These lead artifacts are also recognized by all involved as belonging to the historical heritage of the country of Malta.

As of the printing of this book, the fate of the surviving anchors are as follows:

Two of the anchors have been turned over to officials at the Malta Museum, generous gifts given in memory of Tony by his wife Margaret and his friend Charles Grech.

The family of "Mario the diver" is involved in meaningful dialogue to determine an appropriate disposition of that ancient treasure.

And the weathered dive weight that had been melted down from the torn-in-half anchor found by Tony and Ray sits in front of me as I type these final words—the chiseled "MT" indelibly etched on its dull gray surface.

A presidential pardon has been signed by the President and Prime Minister of Malta, giving amnesty to those persons who possessed the anchor stocks found on the seabed in St. Thomas Bay. The order from the President is as follows:

ORDNI

MILL-PRESIDENT TA' MALTA

LIL KULL MIN HUWA KONĊERNAT

BILLI ġie rakkomandat lili mill-Ministru responsabbli għall-Kultura illi tingħata maħfra lill-persuni illi għandhom fill-pussess tagħhom oġġetti ta' antikità li għandhom importanza ġeoloġika, paleontoliġika, arkeoloġika, ta' qdumija jew artistika misjuba f'kull żmien f'qiegħ il-baħar fl-ibħra territorjali Maltin inkluż is-sikka tal-Munxar fil-Bajja ta' San Tumas limiti ta' Marsaskala Malta, u li qeghdin iżommu l-istess oġġetti bi ksur ta' l-Att dwar il-Protezzjoni tal-Antikitajiet (Kap 54) jew ta' l-Att Dwar il-Patrimonju Kulturali (Kap 445) jew ta' xi liġi oħra u illi din il-maħfra tingħata taħt il-kondizzjoni illi l-oġġetti imsemmija jiġu ritornati, konsenjati u permanentement ċeduti bla ħlas lill-Gvern, jew direttament mill-persuni illi għandhom dawk l-oġġetti jew permezz ta' xi intermedjarju, sa mhux aktar tard minn sittin (60) jum mid-data ta' din il-maħfra, u dan sabiex tingħata l-opportunità illi l-istess oġġetti jidħlu fil-pussess ta' l-awtoritajiet inkarigati illi jieħdu ħsieb il-wirt storiku u antikwarju Malti u dawn il-każijiet jiġu riżolti.

U BILLI jiena naqbel ma' din ir-rakkomandazzjoni.

JIENA ISSA GĦALHEKK, Guido de Marco, President ta' Malta, bis-saħħa tas-setgħat mogħtija lili bl-Artikolu 93 tal-Kostituzzjoni,
B'DAN NORDNA li tingħata maħfra lill-persuni li fi żmien sittin (60) jum mid-data ta' din il-maħfra jirritornaw, jikkonsenjaw u permanentement iċedu bla ħlas lill-Ministru responsabbli għall-Kultura, direttament jew permezz ta' intermedjarju, oġġetti ta' antikità li għandhom importanza ġeoloġika, paleontoloġika, arkeoloġika, ta' qdumija jew artistika misjuba f'kull żmien f'qiegħ il-baħar fl-ibħra territorjali Maltin inkluż is-sikka tal-Munxar fil-Bajja ta' San Tumas limiti ta' Marsaskala, Malta illi huma jkunu iddetjenew bi ksur ta' l-Att dwar il-Protezzjoni tal-Antikitajiet (Kap 54) jew ta' l-Att dwar il-Patrimonju Kulturali (Kap 445) jew ta' xi liġi oħra u dan rigward kull reat u/jew kull responsabilità kriminali riżultanti mill-istess detenzjoni, sejbien jew tfittxija ta' l-oġġetti in kwistjoni.

Din l-ordni tibda sseħħ fil- **23** ta' Vattembru 2002.

U għal dan il-għan din hija awtorità biżżejjed

Magħmul il-Palazz, Valletta
Illum **23** ta' Settembru tas-sena
Elfejn u tnejn

PRESIDENT TA' MALTA

B'AWTORITÀ

PRIM MINISTRU

To whom it may concern:

Since it has been recommended by the Minister responsible for Culture, that a presidential pardon be granted to those persons who have in their possession antique objects having a geological, palaeontological, archaeological, antiquarian or artistic importance, found during any time in the seabed in St. Thomas Bay limits of Marsascala, Malta and who are detaining, maintaining the said objects in breach of the Antiquities (Protection) Act (Chapter 54) or the Cultural Heritage Act (Chapter 445) or of any other law and that the said presidential pardon be granted under the condition that the items mentioned be returned, consigned and permanently handed over to the Minister responsible for culture, whether directly by the persons who are in possession of the said objects or through intermediaries, 60 days from the date of this pardon, and this so as to give the opportunity for the competent authorities be given possession of the said objects, which authorities are responsible for Maltese Cultural Heritage and antiquarian, and this in order to resolve these cases.

And since I agree with the above recommendation.

I, Gwido De Marco, President of Malta, therefore, in virtue of the powers given to me by Section 93 of the Maltese Constitution, hereby order that a pardon is granted to those persons who, within 60 days from the date of this presidential pardon, return, consign and permanently hand over to the Minister responsible for Culture, directly or through intermediaries, objects having a geological, palaeontological, archaeological, antiquarian or artistic importance, found during any time in the seabed in St. Thomas Bay limits of Marsascala, Malta and who are detaining, maintaining the said objects in breach of the Antiquities (Protection) Act (Chapter 54) or the Cultural Heritage Act (Chapter 445) or of any other law in relation to any offence resulting from the said detention, discovery or research for the said objects.

This order shall be valid as from the 23rd September 2002.
Signed on the 23rd September 2002 by the Prime Minister and the President of Malta.

ACKNOWLEDGMENTS

What started out as a simple project transformed into several years of an intense commitment of time, effort, and money. It became a labor of love. Any successes resulting from my efforts can only be attributed to those who assisted, guided, and encouraged me along the way. Words could never express the deep appreciation I have for the those kind and generous individuals who made this story possible.

TERRY CORNUKE, EDGAR & YVONNE MILES,

JERRY AND GAIL NORDSKOG, BOB YERKES,

DAVID & PENNY BERGLUND, JIM & ROBIN DAPRA,

JIM AND LAURRA FITZGERALD, KATHY PROFFITT,

JASON MILLIKEN, DAVID HALBROOK, KATHERINE LLOYD,

JENNIFER GOTT, PAM LONGO, BARBARA HONTS,

RAY & CAROLE ARDIZZONE, PETE & BARBARA LEININGER,

MIKE & SUSAN BARNES, RON & DEBY ACTON,

KEN DURHAM, J. O. STEWART, DARRELL & SANDY SCOTT,

RON & TISHA HICKS, DOUG SCHERLING,

CHUCK & NANCY MISSLER, PAUL & NANCY CORNUKE,

JERRY ROSE, MARK & ANGELA PHILLIPS,

MITCH YELLEN, DAVE LADELL, GARY SMELTZER,

JEAN FRANCOIS LAARCHEVEC, GEORGE KRALIK,

BRYAN BOORUJY, DAVID STOTTS, JOHN DOUGLAS,

TOM & KIM BENGARD, GARY & LISA BACKSTROM,

LIONEL CASSON, JIM & PENNY CALDWELL,

JOHN & REGINA CORNUKE, JOEL FREEMAN,

ROY KNUTESON, NORM & CAROLE SONJU,

STEVE MEYER, JOSH MCDOWELL, GENE HANSON,

BRUCE HENDERSON, BILL & SUSAN HENRY,

LEN SALVIG, JACOB CAROTTA, JOYCE WILKINS,

HIS EXCELLENCY PROFESSOR GUIDO DE MARCO,

PRIME MINISTER EDDIE FENECH ADAMI, RAY CIANCIO,

JO PALMER, LOUIS GALEA, MICHAEL RAFELO,

MARGARET MICALLEF-BORG, PAUL GUILLAUMIER,

JOANNE MICALLEF, JOE MICALLEF, CHARLIE VELLA,

JOE NAVARRO, OLIVER NAVARRO, CHARLES GRECH,

WILFRED PIRROTTA, GENERAL RUPERT MONTANARO,

MAJOR MANUEL MALLIA, JAMES MULHOLLAND,

JETHRO MULHOLLAND, MRS. "MARIO",

PROFESSOR ANTHONY BONANNO, PAUL PRECA TRAPANI,

JOHN PRECA TRAPANI, ROGER MAGRO, LE LI, SUE,

MICHAEL & EMMA, MARK MICELI FARRUGIA,

MEDITERRANEAN FILM STUDIOS,

HUGH PERALTA, NOELLA GRIMA,

AQUA BUBBLES DIVING SCHOOL,

JAMES REID, KEVIN BRYAN, JOE & NOAH RITCHIE,

HEATHER MERCER, DAYNA CURRY,

LINDY BOOK, MARY IRWIN VICKERS,

JOHN & REBECCA JACKSON, MISGANNA,

JOHN MCGEE, RON & ANN NEILSON, MARK BRIGHT,

BRETT & JAMIE RUDOLPH, ELIZABETH RIDENOUR,

DIANA SCHNIEDER, LARRY WILLIAMS,

BOB & CAROL WALLACE, BILL & NANCY ZARELLA,

AL & RONNIE FUSTER, PAUL FEINBERG

NOTES

1. Comm. Salvino Athony Scicluna. K. M., *Shipwreck of St. Paul: Conclusions of Underwater Researches by the Malta Underwater Archaeological Branch of the International Institute of Mediterranean Underwater Archaeology, Teams from the Royal Navy, the Royal Air Force, and the Army. 1961-85* (Malta, 1985), 18.

2. Giueseppe Castelli and Charles Cini, *Malta Romana Il Patrimonio Archeologico Delle Isole Maltesi* (1992), 25. "Salina Bay too must have served as a small harbour since it appears to have hosted some harbour activity in antiquity judging from a number of lead anchors in or just outside it."

3. Ibid., 26–8.

4. The explorations focused on two prime areas of St. Paul's Bay: Mistra Bay and Tal Azzenin. The findings, summarized in the published report titled *In Search of St. Paul* by Specialists Archaeological Systems, Malta, revealed nothing relating to first-century shipping or shipwrecks in Mistra Bay. Concerning Tal Azzenin, the report concluded that "…the conditions necessary for a wrecking to occur on Tal Azzenin combined with the type of storm necessary to take ships on the reef would be rarer than immediately expected. Any ship would have already had to negotiate either a passage around St. Paul's Islands or around Qawra Point, and the nonce in the relative security of the bay be brought on to the reef." There have also been theories about Qawra Point—also situated along the same familiar coastline—but numerous problems eliminate its consideration. Not only would the coastline features have been easily recognized by sailors accustomed to navigating by visual reckoning rather than maps; its seafloor contours do not match the depth soundings recorded by Luke as the ship approached the island. As recorded in the Specialists Archaeological Systems report, "The situation of the topography

of the area, combined with the shallow depth of less than five metres for at least one hundred metres around much of the promontory, suggest that this would have seen the foundering of many ships.... The nature of the seabed and the scatter of durable artifacts over a wide area suggest that many ships [and anchors] have been lost [here] in the past." The anchors that have been located in this area are of varying sizes, varying dates, and from depths inconsistent with Luke's record. The evidence is more consistent with a well-visited port outside of which numerous ships throughout the centuries ran aground and sank. A search of nearby Mellieha Bay also produced nothing of significance.

5. Readers Digest, *Strange Stories Amazing Facts* (Readers Digest Association Inc., 1976), 330.

6. See http://members.tripod.com/~S_van_Dorst/legio.html#officers.

7. F. F. Bruce, *Paul: Apostle of the Heart Set Free* (Grand Rapids, Mich.: Wm B. Eerdmans, 1977), 369.

8. Ibid., 368.

9. Lionel Casson, *Ships and Seafaring in Ancient Times* (Austin, Tex.: University of Texas Press, 1994), 124.

10. Ibid., 123.

11. Jefferson White, *Evidence and Paul's Journeys: An Historical Investigation into the Travels of the Apostle Paul* (Hilliard, Ohio: Parsagard Press, 2001), 71.

12. "The Saga of the Lady Be Good" at http://bbs.macmad.org/~jamiecox/ladybegood/ ladybegood.html.

13. *The Great Siege: Passport's Illustrated Guide to Malta and Gozo* (Passports Books, 2000), 90.

14. A. T. Robertson, *A Grammar of the Greek New Testament in the Light of Historical Research* (Nashville, Tenn.: Broadman Press, 1934), 1020–1. This type of construction occurs only eleven times in the New Testament. The

phrase eiv du,nainto appears in Acts 27:39 alone and incorporates the use of ei; plus the optative mood in the protasis, meeting the requirements for a fourth class conditional clause. Earlier in Acts, Luke uses the phrase ei; pwj du,nainto in 27:12, but adds the particle pwj meaning "somehow," indicating that though reaching Phoenix was a "future least probable" long shot, it could still be "somehow" or "in some way" possible. As it turned out, it was not possible.

15. H. G. Liddell and R. Scott, *Greek-English Lexicon* (Oxford, England: Clarendon Press, 1996).

16. Thayer's Lexicon as derived from Grimms Lexicon of 1889.

17. According to *Sport Diving: The British Sub-Aqua Club Diving Manual* (London: Ebury Press, 1993), 146, "The use of compressed air for lifting heavy objects was pioneered by Cox and Danks in Scapa Flow during the 1920s. Vessels as large as 26,000-ton battleships were raised using the natural buoyancy of the upturned ships after the holes had been plugged and they had been filled with air."

18. Another witness to other witnesses described the anchor as literally being cut in two, as if the anchor had been cut by a hacksaw.

19. *Archaeology and Fertility Cult in the Ancient Mediterranean,* and *Religion and Society in the Prehistoric Mediterranean*. Professor Bonanno has also authored various publications on Roman Art and Maltese Archaeology. Among some of the more important are *Malta: An Archaeological Paradise* (Malta, 1987); *Excavations at Hal Millieri, Malta,* a report on the excavation campaign conducted on behalf of the National Museum of Malta (coauthor and coeditor with T. F. C. Blagg and A. T. Luttrell, University of Malta Press, 1990); *Roman Malta: The Archaeological Heritage of the Maltese Islands* (Rome, 1992).

20. *The Harper Collins Atlas of the Bible* (London: Times Books Limited, 1998), 173.

21. Lloyd J. Ogilvie, *The Communicator's Commentary: Acts* (Waco, Tex.: Word Books, 1983), 335.

22. Casson, *Ships and Seafaring in Ancient Times,* 103–4.

23. Synesius, *Epistolae*, 4.160a, as cited in Casson, *Ships and Seafaring in Ancient Times,* 129.

24. Josephus, *The Life of Flavius Josephus*, 3.15, as published in *The New Complete Works of Josephus* (Grand Rapids, Mich.: Kregel Publications, 1999), 18.

25. Alan Millard, *Illustrated Wonders and Discoveries of the Bible* (Nashville, Tenn.: Thomas Nelson), 211.

26. J. D. Douglas, organizing ed., *The New Bible Dictionary* (Grand Rapids, Mich.: Wm B. Eerdmans, 1974), 945.